The All-Of-The-Above Energy Strategy as a Path to Sustainable Economic Growth

Executive Summary..2

I.   Introduction: Elements of the All-of-the-Above Energy Strategy 5

II.   The Energy Revolution and the Economic Recovery 9

        The Energy Revolution in Historical Perspective 9

        GDP, Jobs, and the Trade Deficit...15

        Energy Prices, Households, and Manufacturers 18

III.   The Energy Revolution and Energy Security: A Macroeconomic Perspective 20

        Trends in Oil Import Prices and Shares 21

        Macroeconomic Channels of Oil Price Shocks 22

        Empirical Analysis of Energy Price Shocks 24

            The changing sensitivity of the U.S. economy to oil price shocks 24

            Energy supply diversification and falling correlations among U.S. energy prices 29

        Discussion..29

IV.   A Path to a Low-Carbon Future..31

        Reducing Emissions through Improved Efficiency 32

        Natural Gas as a Transitional Fuel...34

        Supporting Renewables, Nuclear, and Clean Coal 35

            Electricity from Wind and Solar Energy 36

            Other Renewables...37

            Nuclear and Clean Coal 37

            Meeting the Challenge of the Transportation Sector 38

        International Leadership..39

References..41

Executive Summary

The U.S. energy sector is undergoing a profound transformation. The United States is producing more oil and natural gas, is generating more electricity from renewables such as wind and solar, and is consuming less petroleum while holding electricity consumption constant. These developments have had substantial economic and energy security benefits, and they are helping to reduce carbon emissions in the energy sector and thereby tackle the challenge posed by climate change.

To build on this progress, to foster economic growth, and to protect the planet for future generations, the President has set out an aggressive All-of-the-Above strategy on energy. Some of the recent trends in the energy sector predate the Administration and stem from technological advances and risk-taking by American entrepreneurs and businesses, as well as from government-supported research and other public policies. The All-of-the-Above energy strategy supports these trends through environmentally responsible production of oil and natural gas. In addition, the Administration has advanced the growth of energy sources with low or zero carbon emissions through programs that support wind, solar, other renewables, and nuclear, and has also helped to reduce energy demand by promoting energy efficiency. The Administration is also supporting an ambitious program of carbon capture, utilization and storage for coal and natural gas power plants and for industrial facilities.

The All-of-the-Above energy strategy has three key elements: to support economic growth and job creation, to enhance energy security, and to deploy low-carbon energy technologies and lay the foundation for a clean energy future. This report lays out these three elements of the All-of-the-Above energy strategy, and takes stock of the progress that has been made to date and the work that remains to be done.

The recent transformation in the domestic energy sector has been historic.

- **Decades-long trends in energy use are being reversed.** Natural gas consumption has risen 18 percent since 2005. In addition, total energy obtained from wind, solar, and geothermal sources has more than doubled since 2009.

- **Many of these changes are largely unforeseen.** Only eight years ago, baseline projections showed steadily increasing petroleum consumption well into the future. But the Energy Information Administration now projects petroleum consumption to decline starting after 2019. In fact, since its peak in 2007, U.S. gasoline consumption has fallen by 5.5 percent, or half a million barrels per day.

The energy sector has provided key support to the recovery from the Great Recession, and the U.S. economy's exposure to abrupt adverse changes in world oil markets should continue to decline.

- **Rising domestic energy production has made a significant contribution to GDP growth and job creation.** The increases in oil and natural gas production alone contributed more than 0.2 percentage point to real GDP growth in both 2012 and 2013, and employment in these sectors increased by 133,000 between 2010 and 2013. Tens of thousands more jobs have been created in the solar and wind industries. These figures do not account for all the economic spillovers, so the overall impact on the economy of this growth in oil and gas production is even greater.

- **Excluding the crisis-affected year of 2009, the U.S. trade deficit as a percent of GDP is the lowest since the 1990s.** Since its 2006 peak, more than a fifth of the narrowing of the trade deficit as a percent of GDP can be directly attributed to a shrinking trade deficit in petroleum products, as rising domestic production and declining domestic consumption have combined to cut oil imports.

- **The resilience of the economy to international supply shocks—macroeconomic energy security—is enhanced by reducing spending on net petroleum imports and by reducing oil dependence.** The factors that have reduced net oil imports—decreased domestic petroleum demand, increased domestic oil production, more efficient vehicles, and increased use of biofuels—reduce the vulnerability of the U.S. economy to oil price shocks stemming from international supply disruptions. Although international oil supply shocks and oil price volatility will always present risks, empirical evidence presented in this report suggests that further reductions in net petroleum imports will reduce those risks.

- **The United States has emerged as the world's leading producer of petroleum and natural gas.** In 2013, combined production of petroleum, natural gas, and other liquid fuels in the United States exceeded that of Saudi Arabia and Russia. The United States leads in natural gas and is predicted by the International Energy Agency to lead in oil as well within a few years.

The President's All-of-the-Above Energy Strategy will sustain and strengthen this important progress, while deploying low-carbon technologies and laying the foundation for a clean energy future.

- **The United States has reduced its total carbon pollution since 2005 more than any other nation on Earth.** While energy-related CO_2 emissions have fallen 10 percent from their peak in 2007, recent projections suggest that emissions could begin to increase again, and more work remains to address this critical imperative. In his 2013 State of the Union address, the President again called on Congress to pass legislation that would provide a market-based mechanism for reducing emissions. Absent a market-based solution, a central goal of national energy policy is to develop and to deploy low-carbon technologies that the market would not otherwise undertake because of the externality of greenhouse gas emissions.

- **The President's All-of-the-Above Energy Strategy embraces natural gas as a transitional fuel, and includes steps to ensure that natural gas development is done responsibly.** Natural gas is comparatively cleaner than many other sources of energy. And while extraction of natural gas raises some environmental concerns, including fugitive methane emissions, the Administration is supporting safe and responsible development including a strategy to address gaps in current data on methane emissions, to reduce "upstream" methane emissions, and—as part of the Quadrennial Energy Review—to identify "downstream" methane reduction opportunities.

- **The All-of-the-Above Energy Strategy supports renewables, nuclear, and other zero-carbon energy sources through research, development, and deployment, and also invests in energy efficiency.** The Interior Department is on track to permit enough renewable energy projects on public lands by 2020 to power more than six million homes; the Defense Department has set a goal to deploy three gigawatts of renewable energy— including solar, wind, biomass, and geothermal—on Army, Navy, and Air Force installations by 2025; as part of the Climate Action Plan, the Federal Government committed to sourcing 20 percent of the energy consumed in Federal buildings from renewable sources by 2020; and the Energy Department supports clean energy technology development and cost reduction across the innovation chain, including through significant loan guarantees and demonstration projects to promote nuclear, renewables, efficiency, and clean coal technologies.

I. Introduction: Elements of the All-of-the-Above Energy Strategy

Over the past ten years, the U.S. economy has undergone a revolution in the production and consumption of energy. Breakthroughs in nonconventional oil and natural gas extraction technology have reversed the decades-long decline in domestic oil and natural gas production. The composition of energy sources has begun to shift: petroleum and coal are now being replaced by natural gas and renewables, cleaner sources with low or zero carbon emissions.

Some of these trends predate the Administration, and the President's All-of-the-Above energy strategy supports these trends and aims to accelerate them in an environmentally responsible way. Other trends are newer, and are driven in part by the President's policies.

The President's All-of-the-Above energy strategy has three key elements: to support economic growth and job creation, to enhance energy security, and to deploy low-carbon technologies and lay the foundation for a clean energy future. This report lays out these three elements of the All-of-the-Above Energy Strategy, and takes stock of the progress that has been made to date and the work that remains to be done.

The energy sector has provided key support to the recovery from the Great Recession. Today, as shown in Figure 1-1, the United States produces more crude oil than it imports. Natural gas production has climbed sharply and natural gas prices have fallen, to the benefit of industry and consumers. Employment in the oil and natural gas extraction sector increased by 133,000 from 2010 to 2013. Many more jobs have been added in sectors that support activity in extractive industries like manufacturing, transportation, construction, restaurants and lodging, as well as local jobs in schools, grocery stores, hospitals, and other establishments in drilling regions. And even more jobs have been induced by the extra spending created by these jobs, given the elevated rate of unemployment during the recovery. The CEA estimates that oil and gas extraction alone contributed 0.2 percentage point to GDP growth in 2012 and 2013—and this large contribution does not include all the economic spillovers. The decline in net petroleum imports has helped to reduce the U.S. trade deficit. And the dramatic growth in renewable electricity generating capacity, especially in wind and solar, has also boosted employment and output during the recovery.

Figure 1-1
U.S. Crude Oil Production and Net Imports

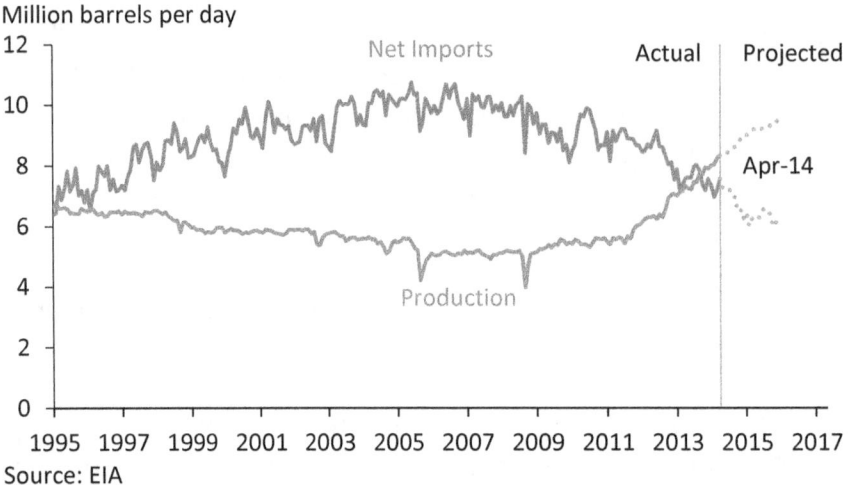

Source: EIA

The energy revolution is also making the United States more energy secure. Declining net imports reduce the macroeconomic vulnerability of the United States to foreign oil supply disruptions. In today's deregulated domestic liquid fuels market and globally integrated oil market, an international supply disruption means a jump in prices because of the inelastic short-run demand for oil. But the combination of declining gasoline consumption, increasing domestic crude oil production, increasing fuel economy, and increasing use of biofuels enhances the resilience of the U.S. economy to these oil price shocks. Although international oil supply shocks and oil price volatility will always present risks, empirical evidence presented in this report suggests that reductions in net petroleum imports will reduce those risks. Ultimately, long-term reductions of net oil imports must come from reduced demand and increased use of biofuels, electric vehicles, natural gas, and other substitutes for petroleum in transportation. In addition, the diversification of energy sources through the growth of natural gas and renewables has softened the link between world oil prices and domestic energy prices.

The President's All-of-the-Above energy strategy is also developing and deploying low-carbon technologies and laying the foundation for a clean energy future. From 2005 through 2011 (the last year of data), the United States reduced its total carbon pollution more than any other nation on Earth, in part because of a shift in the United States towards cleaner natural gas and an increasing role for renewables. Although the reductions in CO_2 emissions so far are an historic shift from past trends, more work remains, and business-as-usual projections still suggest that CO_2 emissions will increase over the rest of this decade as the economy grows. These increasing emissions impose economic and other costs on generations to come—in other words, carbon-intensive energy consumption generates a negative externality that affects the welfare of today's population and their children. Imposing these costs on future generations is irresponsible and our current business-as-usual path is unacceptable.

The President's All-of-the-Above energy strategy makes progress on addressing this critical issue. Natural gas has the lowest CO_2 emissions per unit of usable energy produced of any fossil fuel.

Switching from fuels with a greater carbon footprint to natural gas has played a vital role in decarbonizing the energy sector, and will continue to do so for the coming decades. To ensure a small greenhouse gas footprint for natural gas, the Administration is working with States and industry to address the challenges of fugitive emissions of methane (a potent greenhouse gas) and flaring. In addition, through the Department of Energy and the Quadrennial Energy Review, the Administration will identify "downstream" methane reduction opportunities. Renewables will play a central role in a low-carbon energy future. The All-of-the-Above energy strategy supports programs that help to bring down costs of those renewables approaching market readiness, for example through solar programs such as the Department of Energy's SunShot initiative. Absent a comprehensive market-based solution that internalizes the externality posed by carbon emissions, the All-of-the-Above strategy also entails working towards the outcomes of such a solution through policies that include new energy efficiency standards, a continuation of the Renewable Electricity Production Tax Credit, an extended cellulosic fuel tax credit, and direct regulation of carbon emissions.

The Box summarizes some key Administration initiatives under the All-of-the-Above energy strategy.

Electricity

- Issued about $30B in DOE loan guarantees: kickstarted utility-scale solar; supported "first mover" advanced nuclear reactors with enhanced safety features in Georgia; enabled auto industry to retool for very efficient and electric vehicles.
- In partnership with industry, invested in four commercial-scale and 24 industrial-scale clean coal projects that will store more than 15 million metric tons of CO_2 per year.
- Under the American Recovery and Reinvestment Act, supported more than 90,000 projects by leveraging nearly $50 billion in private, regional, and state dollars to deploy enough renewable electricity to power 6.5 million homes annually.
- As part of a commitment to improvements in permitting and transmission for renewables, approved 50 utility-scale renewable energy proposals and associated transmission, including 27 solar, 11 wind, and 12 geothermal projects since 2009, enough to power 4.8 million homes. Thirteen of the projects are already in operation.

Transportation

- In 2011, finalized national standards to double the efficiency of light-duty cars and trucks by 2025, reducing oil consumption by 2.2 million barrels a day in 2025 and slashing greenhouse gas emissions by 6 billion metric tons over the lifetime of the vehicles sold during this period.
- Building on the first-ever medium- and heavy-duty vehicle fuel economy standards released in 2011, began collaborating with industry to develop standards for vehicles beyond model year 2018, which will lead to large savings in fuel, lower CO_2 emissions, and health benefits from reduced particulate matter and ozone.

Energy Efficiency

- Since June 2013 alone, issued proposed or final energy conservation standards for eleven products through the Department of Energy. These standards—when taken together with the final rules already issued under this Administration—mean that more than 70 percent of the President's goal of reducing carbon pollution through appliance efficiency standards will be achieved. As a result, by 2030, CO_2 emissions will fall by at least 3 billion metric tons cumulatively and save hundreds of billions of dollars in energy costs.
- Launched the Better Buildings Challenge in 2011 to help American commercial and industrial buildings become at least 20 percent more energy efficient by 2020. More than 190 diverse organizations, representing over 3 billion square feet, 600 manufacturing plants and close to $2 billion in energy efficiency financing stepped up to the President's Challenge. This year, 25 new states, cities, school districts, multifamily housing, retailers, food service, hospitality and manufacturing organizations announced they are joining as partners.
- Set an additional $2 billion goal in federal energy efficiency upgrades to Federal buildings over the next 3 years. This challenge, in combination with the initial commitment of $2 billion in 2011, will result in a total of $4 billion in energy efficiency performance contracts in the Federal sector through 2016.
- Beginning in 2009, created weatherization programs that helped low-income households save $250-$500 a year on their energy bills and have provided energy efficiency improvements to nearly 2 million homes.

Oil and Natural Gas

- Worked to reduce processing time for onshore drilling permits, now at the lowest it has been in eight years. In FY 2013, onshore production on Federal and Indian lands increased 37% compared with FY 2008. This year, the Interior Department has already held eight onshore lease sales, generating over $78 million in revenue for States, Tribes, and the American taxpayer.
- Promoted environmentally responsible development of offshore resources through the Interior Department's Five-Year Outer Continental Shelf Oil & Gas Leasing Program. Since the implementation of new safety standards following the Deepwater Horizon incident in 2010, the Interior Department has issued 260 new shallow-water well permits and 229 new deep water well permits.

In addition to policies already undertaken, the President, as part of his FY 2015 Budget, has proposed new initiatives including:

- Investing $5.2 billion in funding for clean energy technology activities at the Department of Energy, including $860 million for programs and infrastructure that support nuclear energy technologies, $700 million to increase affordability and convenience of advanced vehicles and renewable fuels, and $400 million in cleaner energy from fossil fuels.
- Establishing an Energy Security Trust to help fund efforts to shift cars and trucks off of petroleum products, a $2 billion investment over 10 years that will support R&D into a range of cost-effective technologies.
- Putting $839 million towards advancing the goals of the Global Climate Change Initiative (GCCI) and the President's Climate Action Plan by supporting bilateral and multilateral engagement with major and emerging economies.

II.   The Energy Revolution and the Economic Recovery

The recent changes in the energy sector and their consequences for economic growth have been remarkable. Increasing production of oil, natural gas, and renewable energy has contributed to employment and GDP growth during the recovery, and declining net petroleum imports have helped to reduce the U.S. trade deficit.

The Energy Revolution in Historical Perspective

Over the past two centuries, the amount of energy consumed in the United States has increased dramatically and its mix has changed to sources of energy that are more potent and more convenient. As Figure 2-1 shows, through the middle of the nineteenth century, the main energy source in the U.S. was wood. The use of coal rose sharply through the early twentieth century, then reached a plateau until its use increased in the 1970s for electricity generation. For most of the twentieth century, petroleum consumption grew sharply, dropping off temporarily after the oil crises of the 1970s but then resuming its growth. Natural gas consumption grew during the second half of the twentieth century and has been used increasingly in homes and industry, and to meet peak electricity demand. During the last quarter of the twentieth century, nuclear electricity generation increased to the point that it now supplies 19 percent of electricity, and wood, the original biofuel, saw a small regional resurgence (primarily for home heating) as a result of the increases in home heating oil prices in the 1970s. Meanwhile, renewables production – which includes biomass and biofuels, hydroelectric, wind, solar, and geothermal energy – has surpassed nuclear energy production.

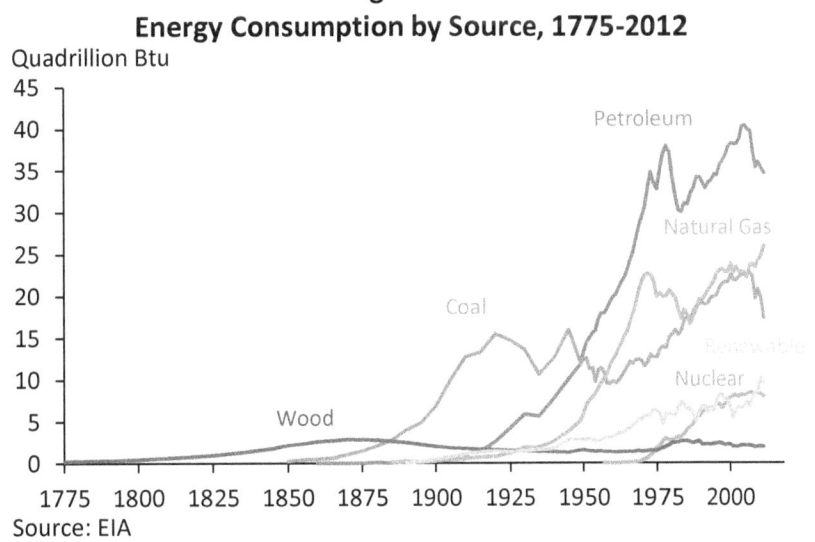

Figure 2-1
Energy Consumption by Source, 1775-2012

Source: EIA

These trends have shifted dramatically in the 21st century: the use of coal has declined by 21 percent since its peak in 2005 and total petroleum consumption has declined by 13 percent since its peak in 2005. Because of the revolution in nonconventional natural gas extraction through horizontal drilling and hydraulic fracturing, natural gas consumption has increased sharply, with much of this increase displacing coal for electricity generation. In addition, total energy obtained from wind, solar, and geothermal sources has increased five-fold since 2005.

The decline in petroleum consumption starting in 2006 was unexpected. A standard way to quantify unforeseen developments is to look at revisions to forecasts, because those revisions represent the contribution of new, unforeseen information. In the case of energy, industry-standard benchmark forecasts are produced annually by the Energy Information Administration (EIA) in its Annual Energy Outlook, so revisions to those forecasts quantify the effect of unforeseen developments on the energy sector. Figure 2-2a shows U.S. petroleum consumption since 1950 and forecasted consumption from the 2006, 2010, and 2014 Annual Energy Outlooks. Only eight years ago, these benchmark forecasts projected increasing petroleum consumption over a thirty-year forecast horizon. But events, including the Great Recession—unforeseen at the time of the EIA's 2006 forecasts—unfolded rapidly: by 2010, EIA had reduced both the level and rate of growth of the forecast, and its 2014 outlook now projects petroleum consumption to decline after a slight increase over the next five years. This unforeseen reversal in petroleum demand is led by the reversal in gasoline demand, which is shown in Figure 2-2b: the 2014 EIA projection of consumption in 2030 is 45 percent below the EIA projection made in 2006. The initial decline in the level of consumption is due in part to the recession, but much of the lower projection for the coming decades reflects unforeseen efficiency improvements stemming from the 2012 light-duty vehicle fuel economy standards, along with some projected switching to diesel in the light-duty fleet.

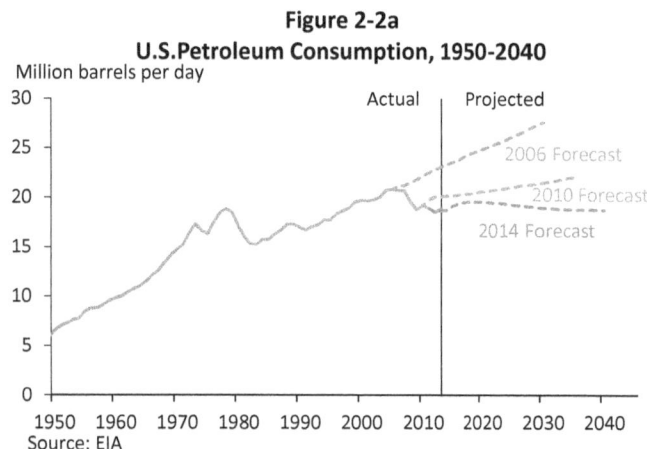

Figure 2-2a
U.S.Petroleum Consumption, 1950-2040
Source: EIA

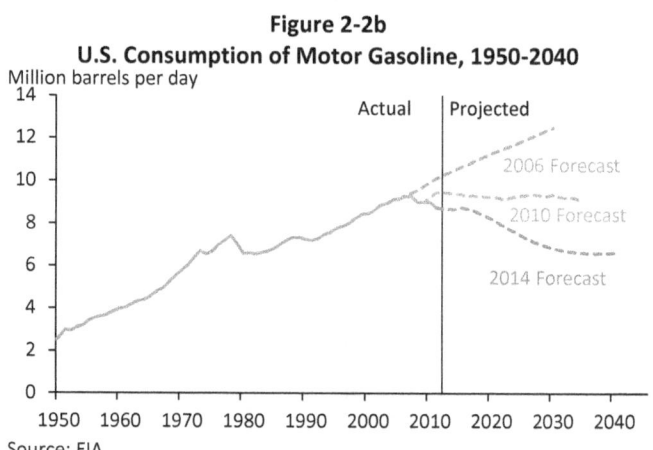

Figure 2-2b
U.S. Consumption of Motor Gasoline, 1950-2040
Source: EIA

The recent increase in petroleum production was equally unforeseen. As Figure 2-3 shows, domestic petroleum production peaked in 1972 at 11 million barrels per day (bpd). Production plateaued through the mid-1980s and then declined steadily through the late 2000s as conventional domestic deposits were depleted. Since then, however, entrepreneurs adapted horizontal drilling and hydraulic fracturing technology that had been more widely used for natural gas, enabling them to extract oil within the rocky formations of plays once considered exhausted, as in the Eagle Ford in West and South Texas, and to develop new plays as in the

Bakken in North Dakota. These developments are both unforeseen and recent: most of the revision to EIA's forecast occurred since 2010, and now EIA projects production to surpass its earlier peak in 2015. EIA projects production to decline slowly after 2019, although because the technology is still advancing there is considerable uncertainty about the economically recoverable resource potential.

Figure 2-3
U.S. Petroleum Production, 1950-2040

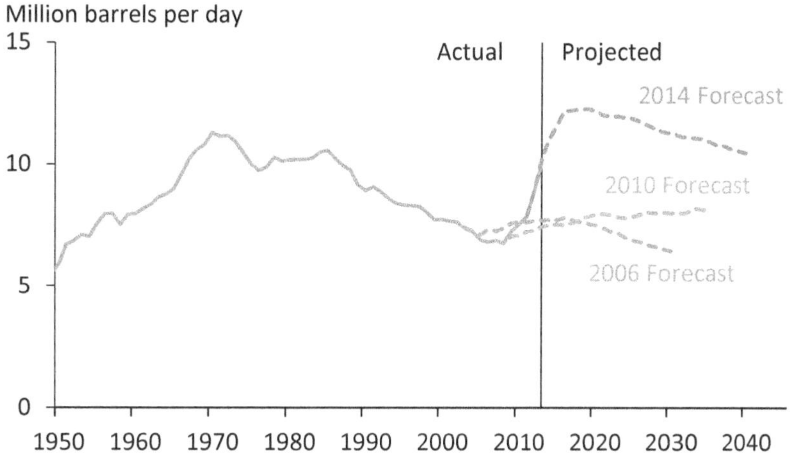

Source: EIA

The unforeseen decline in demand for petroleum and increase in oil production has led to a sharp turnaround in net petroleum imports (Figure 2-4), which fell from a peak of over 12 million bpd in 2005 to 6.2 million bpd in 2013—a drop of more than 6 million bpd in 2013, relative to EIA's 2006 forecast of 2013 imports.[1] Of this unforeseen fall in net imports, roughly 4 million bpd, or 65 percent, is due to the unforeseen fall in consumption, and 2 million bpd, or 35 percent, is due to the unforeseen increase in production, relative to the respective 2006 EIA forecasts.

---

[1] Throughout the focus is on net imports. Although crude exports are restricted by law and have been historically small quantities, the United States has long exported refined petroleum products, for example averaging approximately 750,000 bpd in the 1990s. Refined product exports have grown sharply since 2006, reaching 2.8 million bpd in 2013.

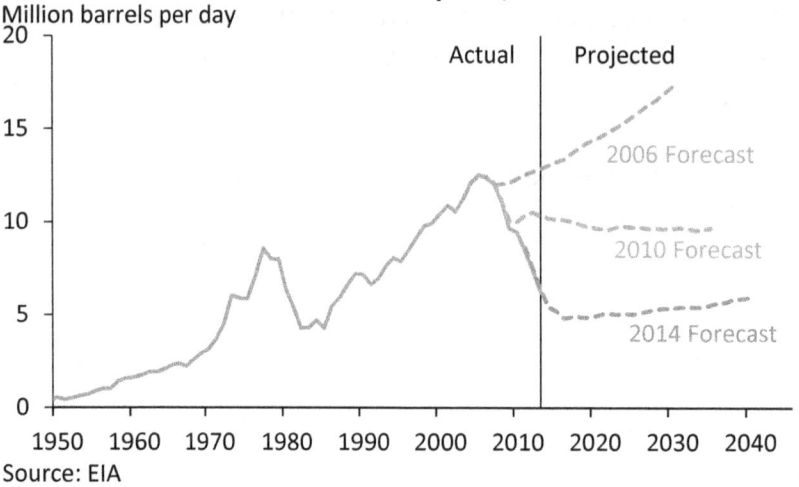

Figure 2-4
U.S. Petroleum Net Imports, 1950-2040

Source: EIA

The increase in nonconventional natural gas production preceded the increase in nonconventional oil production. Figure 2-5, which presents domestic natural gas production and historical EIA forecasts, shows that the EIA's 2014 projections indicate increasing natural gas production through 2040. Already, well over half of natural gas production is from nonconventional plays (tight gas and shale gas), a fraction that is projected to increase as the conventional resource base becomes less productive and competitive.

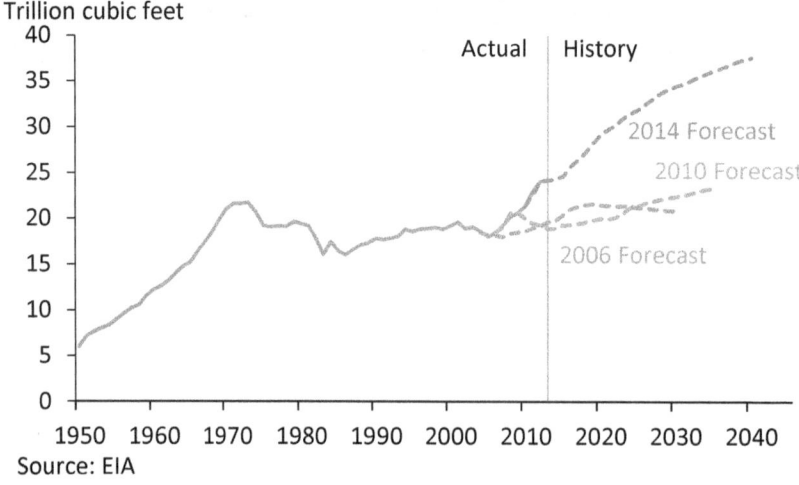

Figure 2-5
U.S. Natural Gas Production, 1950-2040

Source: EIA

Domestic use of renewable energy sources has also increased substantially since 2000. Figure 2-6 shows that the use of liquid biofuels—primarily ethanol from corn and biodiesel from various sources including waste oil and soy oil—grew sharply in the mid-2000s as ethanol replaced MTBE as an oxygenate to boost octane and to reduce emissions of aromatic hydrocarbons, further supported by the Renewable Fuel Standard mandates under the Energy Independence and Security Act of 2007. The combined effect of increased production of natural gas, oil, and liquid biofuels has resulted in the United States being the leading petroleum and natural gas producer in the world (Figure 2-7).

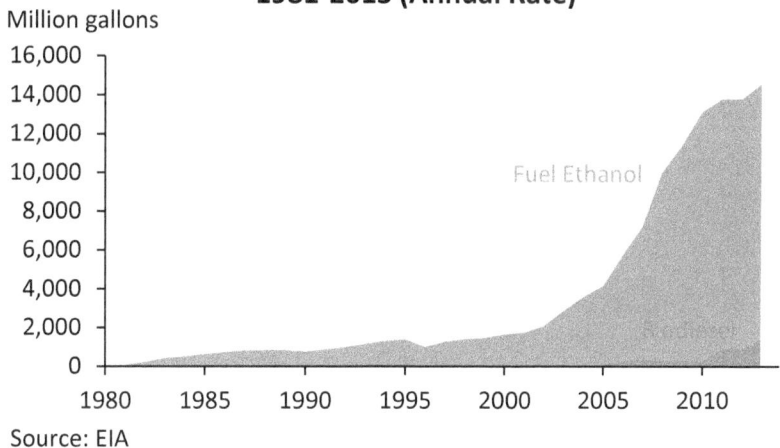

Figure 2-6
U.S. Fuel Ethanol and Biodiesel Consumption,
1981-2013 (Annual Rate)

Source: EIA

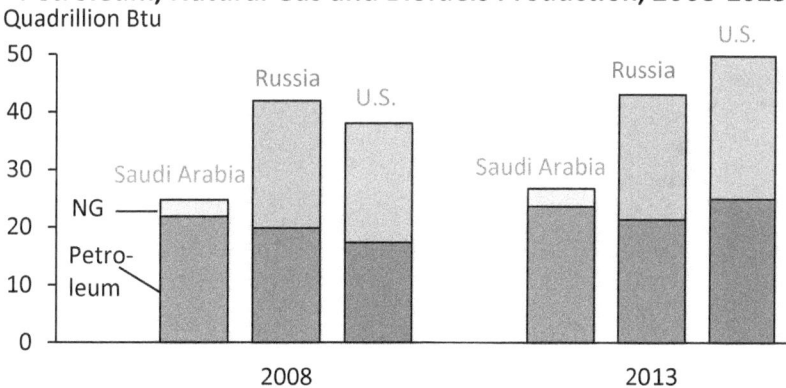

Figure 2-7
Petroleum, Natural Gas and Biofuels Production, 2008-2013

Note: Petroleum production includes crude oil, natural gas liquids, condensates, refinery processing gains and other liquids including biofuels.
Source: EIA

The energy revolution also includes a dramatic increase in the use of renewables. At the end of 2013, wind electricity generation capacity totaled 61 gigawatts, an increase of 140 percent over its 2008 level. In 2012 alone, a record 13 gigawatts of new wind power capacity was installed, roughly double the amount of newly installed capacity in 2011. These 13 gigawatts of new wind capacity represented the largest share of additions by a single fuel source to total U.S. electric generation capacity in 2012. Altogether between 2010 and 2013, total installed wind power generation capacity grew by over 20 gigawatts or 50 percent, with construction throughout the Midwest, Southwest, West Coast, and New England (Figure 2-8). As a result, annual electricity production from wind energy tripled from 2008 to 2013, from 55,363 million kilowatt-hours to 167,567 million kilowatt-hours. Similarly, utility-scale electricity production from solar power grew more than ten-fold from 2008 to 2013, from 864 million kilowatt-hours to 8,918 million kilowatt-hours. Total energy from solar (which in addition to electricity generation includes heating, hot water, and other uses) nearly quadrupled from a monthly rate of 8 trillion Btu to 29 trillion Btu over the same period (Figure 2-9).

Figure 2-8
Change in Wind Power Generation Capacity, 2010-2013

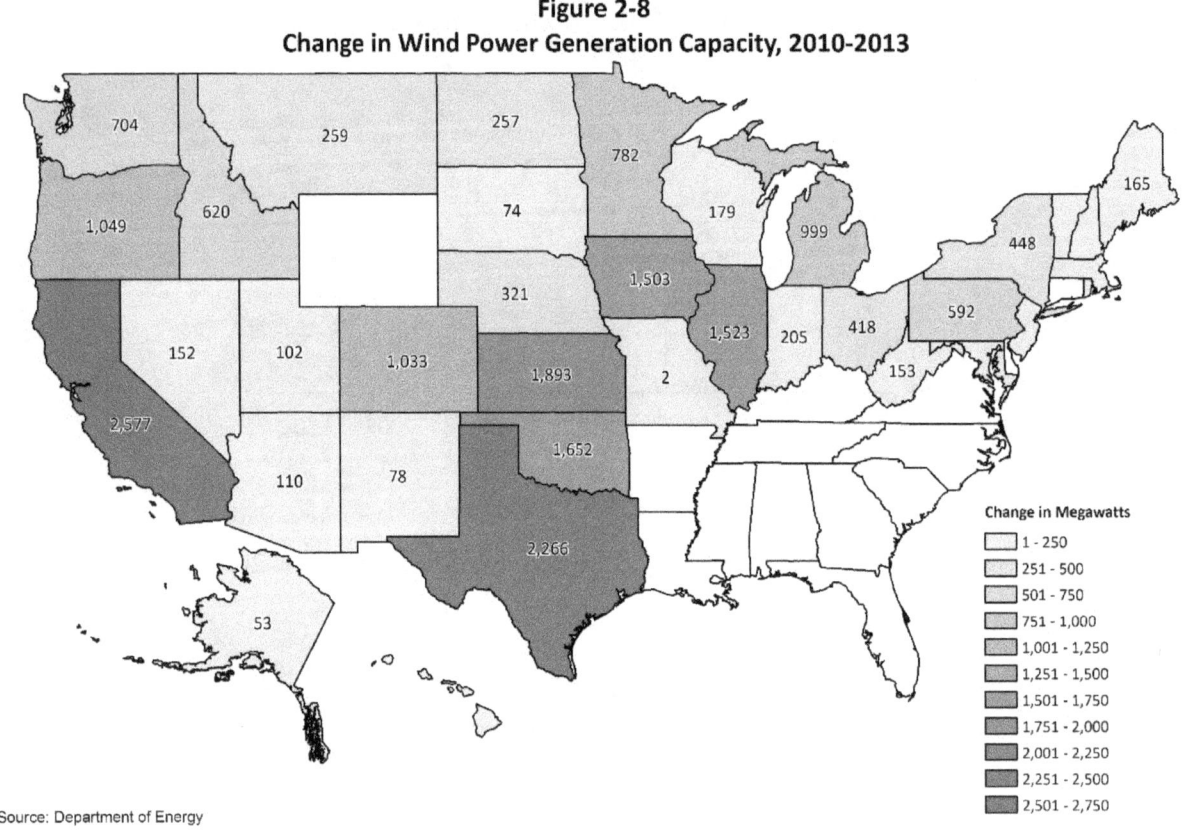

Source: Department of Energy

Figure 2-9
Total Monthly Wind and Solar Energy Production

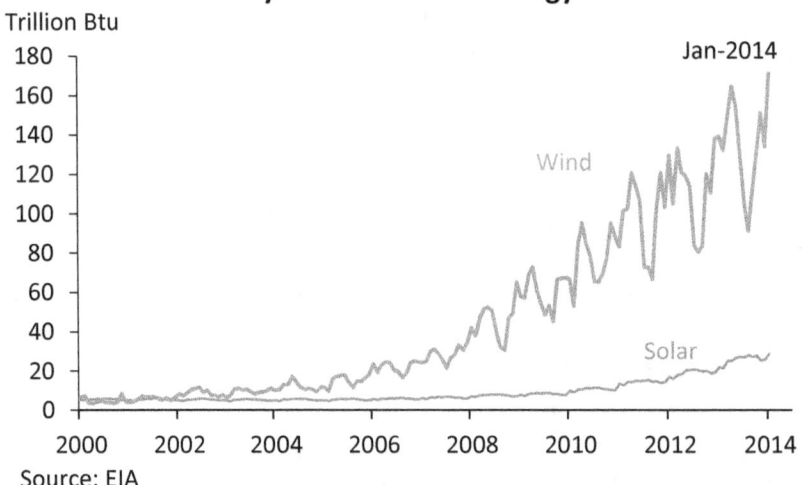

Source: EIA

14

This U.S. energy revolution has contributed to the growth of the economy—both in terms of economic output as measured by gross domestic product (GDP) and overall employment—and the decline of the trade deficit, as the economy recovered from the Great Recession. CEA estimates that the increase in oil and natural gas production alone contributed more than 0.2 percentage point to real GDP growth in both 2012 and 2013, in contrast to a slight negative contribution on average from 1995 to 2005 (Figure 2-10). This 0.2 percentage point contribution, which does not count all the economic spillovers, added substantially to the 2.3 percent annual rate of growth of the economy as a whole over these two years.

Figure 2-10
Contributions of Oil and Natural Gas
Production to GDP Growth

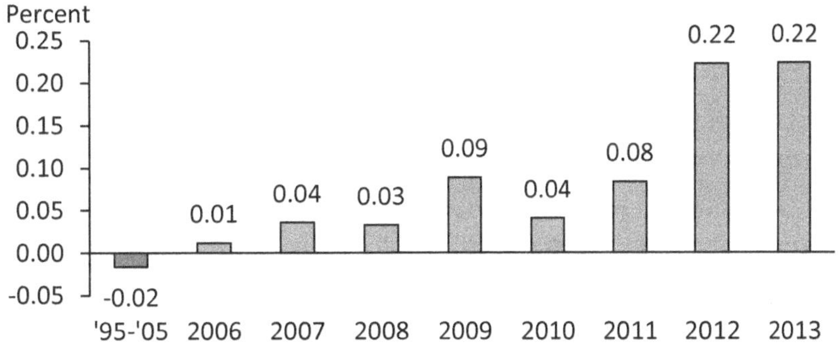

Note: CEA calculations use physical quantity data for oil and natural gas production.
Source: EIA; CEA calculations.

The growth in oil and gas production has both directly and indirectly created jobs over the past several years. As Figure 2-11 shows, employment in the oil and natural gas extraction sector increased by 133,000 between 2010 and 2013, and continues to grow into 2014. Much of this job growth has been concentrated in a handful of states like Texas, Pennsylvania, Louisiana and North Dakota that are at the forefront of developing their energy resources (see Cruz, Smith and Stanley [2014]). In addition to direct employment in resource extraction, jobs have been created in the companies that provide goods and services to those industries and to their workers, including manufacturing, transportation, and leisure and hospitality. Local jobs in schools, retail, health care, and other sectors have also been created in oil and gas development regions. Because of the elevated unemployment rate during the recovery, the number of indirect jobs, including those created through aggregate demand spillovers, could be quite large: one private estimate holds that nonconventional oil and gas activity contributed a total of 1.7 million jobs in 2012 (IHS CERA [2012]). After falling nearly continuously since the early 1980s, employment in coal mining also edged up slightly over this period and in 2012 stood at approximately 90,000 employees.

Figure 2-11
Natural Resource Extraction Employment, 1949-2013

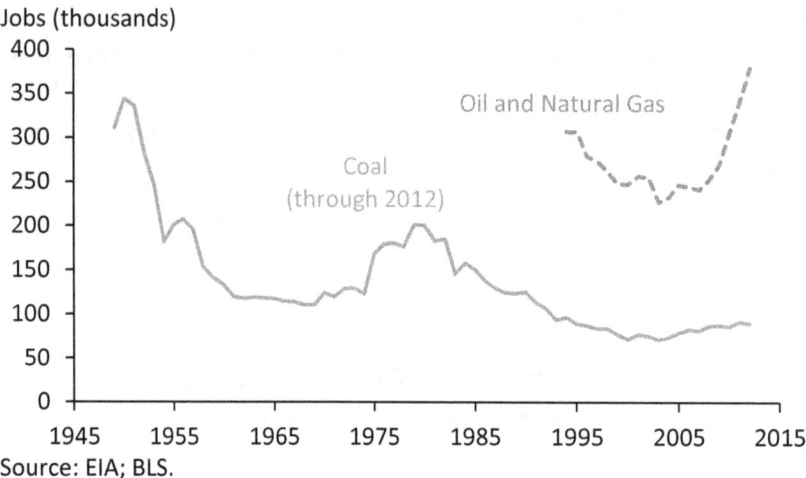

Source: EIA; BLS.

Expansion of renewable energy capacity has also contributed to economic growth. Employment in the renewable sector spans several categories in Federal data collection systems, which complicates direct estimation of employment and output in the sector. However, trade association data suggest that, in addition to rapid expansion in output, there has also been a sharp rise in employment. As Figure 2-12 shows, from 2010 to 2013, employment in the solar energy industry grew by more than 50 percent to almost 143,000 jobs. Moreover, employment in the solar industry is projected to increase by another 20,000 in 2014.[2] Similarly, wind industry employment in 2013 totaled in the tens of thousands.[3]

[2] Estimates of national employment related to the solar energy industry from the Solar Foundation's 2013 National Solar Jobs Census. The National Solar Jobs Census uses a statistical survey methodology aligned with the Bureau of Labor Statistics' Quarterly Census of Employment and Wages and Current Employment Statistics surveys.
[3] Estimates of national employment related to the wind power sector from the 2013 American Wind Energy's Association U.S. Wind Industry Annual Market Report.

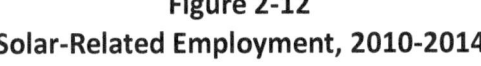

Figure 2-12
Solar-Related Employment, 2010-2014

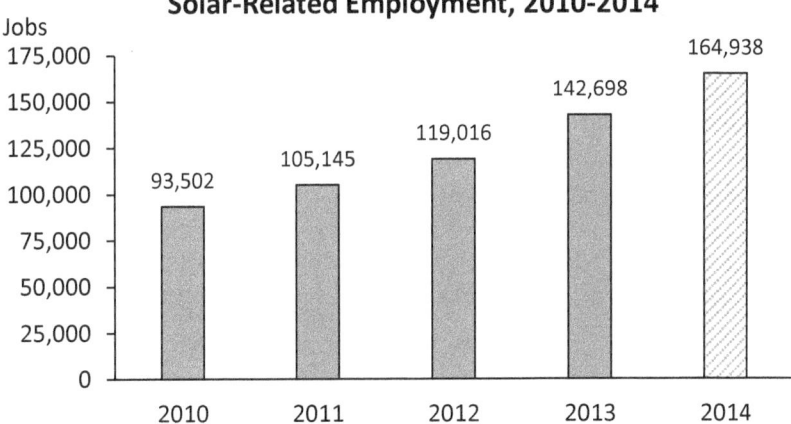

Note: 2014 figure is a projection.
Source: The Solar Foundation

The increase in domestic oil production, combined with reduced demand for oil, has also led to a sharp drop in net petroleum imports and, as a result, a decline in the trade deficit. In 2006, the total trade deficit was 5.4 percent of GDP, the highest recorded for the United States. By the end of 2013, the trade deficit had fallen to 2.8 percent of GDP, which, excluding the crisis-affected year of 2009, was the lowest since 1999 (Figure 2-13). While the U.S. trade balance is subject to a number of influences and depends in large part on economic conditions in other parts of the world, the rise in domestic energy production has been a substantial factor in the recent improvement. Of the 2.6 percentage point decline in the trade deficit since 2006, about 0.6 percentage point (or just over one fifth) is due to a shrinking trade deficit in petroleum products.

Figure 2-13
Total and Petroleum Trade Deficits, 1995-2013

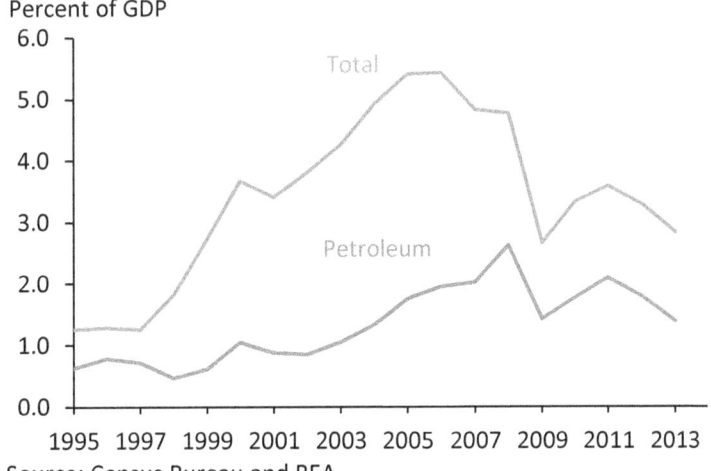

Source: Census Bureau and BEA.

Energy Prices, Households, and Manufacturers

Since 2006, natural gas prices have fallen well below crude oil prices on an energy-equivalent basis, providing a cheaper source of energy to consumers and businesses in the United States (Figure 2-14a). Domestic natural gas prices are also well below those in other countries (Figure 2-14b). Today, one million British thermal units (mmBtu) of wholesale natural gas costs around $4.50, roughly half the price paid in Western Europe, a quarter of the price paid in Japan, and a quarter of the price of a comparable amount of crude oil.[4]

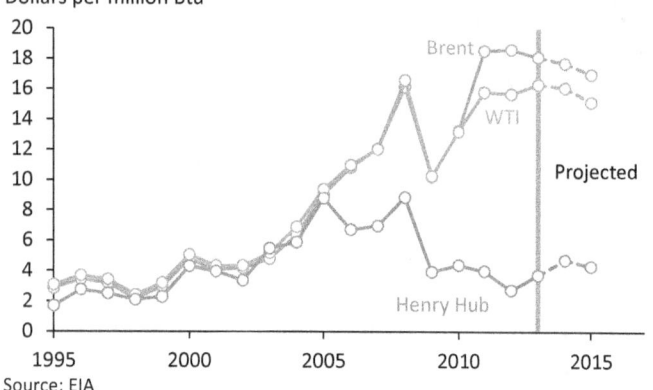

Figure 2-14a
Annual Crude Oil and Natural Gas Spot Prices, 1995-2015
Dollars per million Btu

Source: EIA

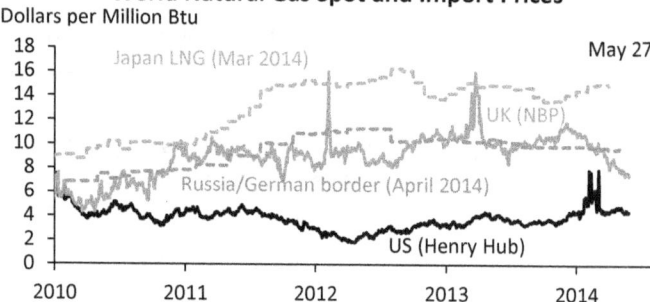

Figure 2-14b
World Natural Gas Spot and Import Prices
Dollars per Million Btu

Note: UK's prices do not include natural gas imported from Russia which is predominately indexed to oil prices. Japan and Russia/German border prices are monthly averages.
Source: Bloomberg

Residential natural gas prices have followed the decline in wholesale natural gas prices, and the twelve-month average price has declined by 20 percent from its 2009 high (Figure 2-15a). Low wholesale natural gas prices have also supported switching fuels in the electric power sector from coal to natural gas. With natural gas prices falling from 2007 to 2012, retail electricity prices have been essentially constant over this period, showing the slowest rate of increase in almost 15 years (Figure 2-15b).

---

[4] The low cost of domestic natural gas relative to other countries reflects the undeveloped nature of international gas markets combined with the expense of transportation. Liquefaction, transportation from the United States to Europe, and regasification have been estimated to add $6-9 per mmBtu, roughly tripling the price of gas entering the pipeline at Europe relative to its Henry Hub price. Currently approximately 9 billion cubic feet per day of liquefied natural gas (LNG) export capacity has been conditionally approved by the Department of Energy, although the enormous capital expenditures required for LNG facilities raises the possibility that some of this capacity might not actually be built. Because of large transport costs, even if a global market for LNG were to develop, domestic natural gas prices are likely to remain well below prices in the rest of the world for an extended period of time.

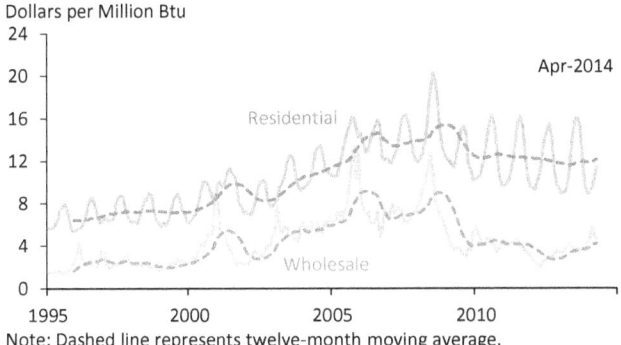

Figure 2-15a
Wholesale and Residential Natural Gas Prices, 1995-2014

Dollars per Million Btu

Apr-2014

Residential

Wholesale

Note: Dashed line represents twelve-month moving average.
Source: EIA

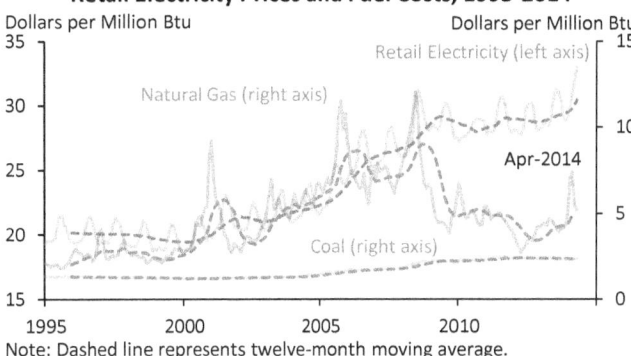

Figure 2-15b
Retail Electricity Prices and Fuel Costs, 1995-2014

Dollars per Million Btu   Dollars per Million Btu

Retail Electricity (left axis)

Natural Gas (right axis)

Apr-2014

Coal (right axis)

Note: Dashed line represents twelve-month moving average.
Source: EIA

III. The Energy Revolution and Energy Security: A Macroeconomic Perspective

The term energy security is used to mean different things in different contexts, and broadly covers energy supply availability, reliability, affordability, and geopolitical considerations.[5] This section focuses on macroeconomic energy security, by which we mean the extent to which a country's economic welfare is exposed to energy supply risks, specifically, international energy supply disruptions that lead to product unavailability or price shocks or both. This concept of macroeconomic energy security encompasses domestic risks as well as international supply risks such as disruptions to foreign oil production. In the United States, domestic energy security considerations are important and domestic supply breakdowns can have large costs. For example, the Council of Economic Advisers and the Department of Energy, as well as others, have estimated substantial costs of electricity grid outages associated with storms (CEA/DOE 2013). In its Quadrennial Energy Review, the Department of Energy is broadly examining the U.S. energy infrastructure to identify potential threats, risks, and opportunities for improvement. Historically, however, energy supply disruptions of foreign origin have had the greatest overall macroeconomic impact, notably international oil supply disruptions played a role in the recessions of the 1970s, although disagreement remains about the magnitude of that role. For this reason, this report focuses on the vulnerability of the U.S. economy to international energy supply disruptions.

Because 95 percent of U.S. energy import dollars are spent on petroleum, the main threats to U.S. macroeconomic energy security come from international oil supply disruptions. During the OPEC oil embargo of 1973-74, price controls and lack of product led to rationing of gasoline and long queues at service stations. But in today's global oil market with many producers and domestically deregulated petroleum prices in the U.S., petroleum products will still be available in the event of a foreign supply disruption, just at a higher price. Today, macroeconomic energy security concerns the resilience of the U.S. economy to temporary unexpected price hikes—price shocks—of foreign origin.

Historically, temporarily high oil price shocks arising from foreign supply disruptions have cut GDP growth and reduced employment. These events have been studied and debated in depth in the economics literature (starting with Hamilton [1983]; see Hamilton [2009] and Kilian [2008b, 2014] for surveys). Table 3-1 presents a list of the major oil supply disruptions from 1973-2005

---

[5] In a joint statement released May 6, 2014, the G7 energy ministers stated: "We believe that the path to energy security is built on a number of core principles: Development of flexible, transparent and competitive energy markets, including gas markets; Diversification of energy fuels, sources and routes, and encouragement of indigenous sources of energy supply; Reducing our greenhouse gas emissions, and accelerating the transition to a low carbon economy, as a key contribution to enduring energy security; Enhancing energy efficiency in demand and supply, and demand response management; Promoting deployment of clean and sustainable energy technologies and continued investment in research and innovation; Improving energy systems resilience by promoting infrastructure modernization and supply and demand policies that help withstand systemic shocks; [and] Putting in place emergency response systems, including reserves and fuel substitution for importing countries, in case of major energy disruptions."

identified in Kilian (2008a), the estimated gross peak supply loss, and the percentage change in oil prices in the aftermath of the disruption. For example, in the months following the Iranian Revolution in November 1978, oil prices increased by 53 percent. This link is not perfect, and not every oil price shock has led to an economic slowdown, but as is discussed below in more detail, the empirical evidence points to a negative link between oil price spikes and economic activity.

Table 3-1: Major Oil Disruptions, 1973-2005

Event Name	Date	Duration (months)	Gross Peak Supply Loss (millions of barrels per day)	Percent Change in Oil Prices
Arab Oil Embargo & Arab-Israeli War	Oct-73 to Mar-74	6	4.3	45%
Iranian Revolution	Nov-78 to Apr-79	6	5.6	53%
Iran-Iraq War	Oct-80 to Jan-81	3	4.1	40%
Persian Gulf War	Aug-90 to Jan-91	6	4.3	32%
Civil Unrest in Venezuela	Dec-02 to Mar-03	4	2.6	28%
Iraq War	Mar-03 to Dec-03	10	2.3	28%

Note: Events as identified in Kilian (2008a) and Hamilton (2005). Dates and gross peak supply loss figures as identified in IEA(2012). Price changes for events over select windows as specified in Hamilton (2005) and price changes before 1982 measured using crude petroleum PPI as in Hamilton (2005).

Trends in Oil Import Prices and Shares

The price of oil plays central roles in macroeconomic energy security. Figure 3-1 shows the price of oil in nominal (current dollars) and in 2013 dollars (deflated by the price index for consumer spending). Jumps in the price of oil are visible around the disruptions of Table 3-1, as well as more gradual increases such as in 2007-08. In real terms, today's oil prices of roughly $100 per barrel are comparable with those in the late 1970s and early 1980s, but are roughly three times the real prices of the 1990s.

Figure 3-1
Nominal and Real Oil Prices (2013 $)

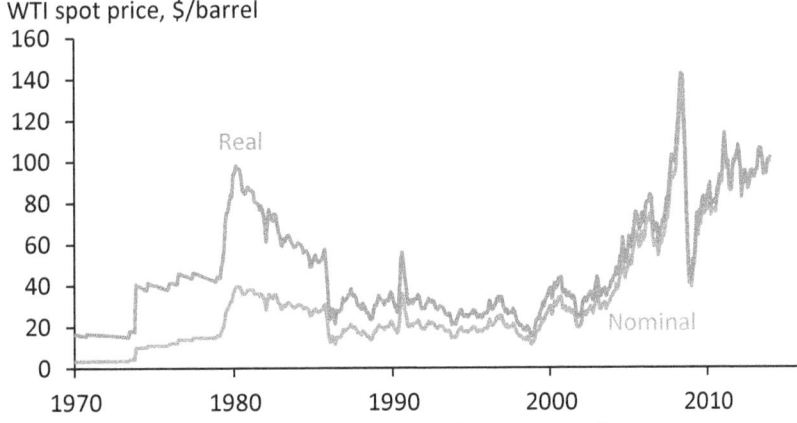

Note: Nominal prices deflated using overall PCE price index.
Source: EIA; Bureau of Economic Analysis.

The expenditure share of net petroleum imports measures the fraction of GDP that is spent on net imports of petroleum. Ignoring compositional differences, this share is the product of net barrels of petroleum imports times the price per barrel, divided by GDP. Figure 3-2 presents two measures of the expenditure share of GDP of net crude imports. The first uses a narrow definition of net imports of crude, gasoline, distillates, and fuel oil. The second, which is only available since 1973, uses a broader definition that includes other refined products (naphtha, jet fuel, etc.) which slightly increases the share relative to the narrow measure but does not materially change the overall time series pattern. In order to observe longer-term movements, the figure also presents a time series trend of the two measures, which reduces the influence of the high frequency fluctuations in these series that arise from short-term price volatility. For example, during the 1990s the price of oil was low even though physical imports were high, so the expenditure share was relatively low. In contrast, the high oil prices of the past few years have produced a relatively high expenditure share, although this share has declined noticeably over the past few years as domestic demand has declined and domestic oil production has increased.

Figure 3-2
Net Import Shares of Petroleum Products

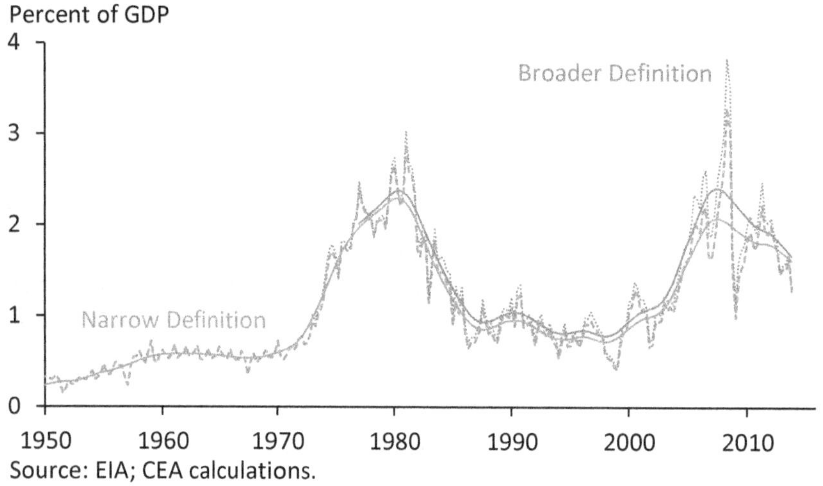

Source: EIA; CEA calculations.

Macroeconomic Channels of Oil Price Shocks

Oil price shocks can affect the economy through several channels, including consumer demand, the supply of goods and services (production), and physical product rationing. As Kilian (2009) and Blinder (2009) point out, these channels are both conceptually distinct and can have different macroeconomic effects.

Because the demand for petroleum products is inelastic, especially in the short run, the share of expenditures by consumers and firms on petroleum goes up when the oil price increases.[6] Because the Unites States is a net importer of oil, expenditures on net imports increase when the oil price increases. If the oil shock is known to be temporary, the life cycle theory of consumption suggests that consumers would make minimal adjustments to the rest of their spending and

---

[6] For example, Kilian and Murphy (2014) estimate the short-run price elasticity of demand for oil to be approximately -0.2, and earlier estimates show even smaller elasticities.

would temporarily finance the additional oil consumption through savings. However, in practice consumers do not know the duration of a price hike and many or most would instead reduce their spending on other goods and services to pay for the more expensive fuel needed for daily life. Because expenditures on oil imports go abroad and not to the domestic economy, they do not count towards GDP, so the immediate effect of an increase in the price of an imported good which, like oil, has inelastic demand, is to decrease consumption of domestic goods and services and thus to decrease GDP. This effect on reducing domestic demand is as if the wealth of consumers were reduced, so this channel is sometimes referred to as the wealth channel. This channel can be large. For example, if net oil imports are 2 percent of GDP, as they were in the late 70s and late 2000s, a 10 percent increase in the price of oil causes a reduction in spending on everything else and reduces GDP by 0.2 percent. The extent to which this channel is offset depends on the source of the oil price increase. For example, an increase in overall world economic activity that drives up the demand for and price of oil would expand U.S. exports, at least partially offsetting the increased price of oil imports.

An oil price increase, like a change in the relative price of any other good, also changes the composition of demand as consumers shift spending from items that are indirectly affected by the price increase (like air travel and cars with low fuel efficiency) to goods and services that are less energy-intensive. Thus, products of energy-intensive sectors become relatively more expensive and those sectors will see a reduction in demand, and even within sectors demand can shift across products, such as to cars with greater fuel efficiency. Moreover, to the extent that shifting from energy-intensive goods reduces purchases of durables such as automobiles or refrigerators, spending today is shifted into the future, depressing aggregate demand. Although this compositional shift increases demand in less energy-intensive sectors, it takes time for displaced workers to find alternative employment so incomes decline and unemployment rises (see for example Hamilton [1988]).

An oil price increase can also depress domestic demand if it increases uncertainty. Uncertainty about the economic future can lead consumers to postpone major purchases and can lead firms to postpone investment and hiring, thereby slowing the economy (e.g. Bernanke [1983], Bloom [2009], and for oil investment specifically, Kellogg [2010]). In this channel, oil price volatility can be causal (the volatility creates uncertainty that postpones investment, hiring, or durables consumption), or the volatility can simply reflect broader market uncertainty about future economic or geopolitical events. Another potential demand-side channel is a fall in aggregate consumption because an oil price rise is regressive and transfers income from individuals with a high marginal propensity to consume to individuals with a lower marginal propensity to consume (e.g. Nordhaus [2007]).

Oil price increases can also reduce economic activity through the supply side of the economy. To the extent that energy prices more broadly move with oil prices, an increase in oil prices makes energy a more expensive factor of production, so firms will strive to reduce energy consumption and expenditures. Although capital and labor substitute for energy in the long run, in the short run they can be complements in production because of fixed technologies, so higher energy costs can result in layoffs in energy-intensive firms and industries. Because it takes time for displaced workers to find jobs, incomes decline and unemployment rises. This supply-side channel matters most if price increases are long-lasting, and because capital and labor are being used less efficiently, could also be associated with a slowdown or decline in productivity growth.

The channels discussed so far all concern changes in the relative price of oil and assume that oil is available. If, however, prices are not flexible and instead oil or petroleum products are rationed, the effect on the economy can be severe. On the production side, because energy and labor are complements in the short run, many workers cannot do their jobs without oil. Time spent queuing for gasoline is time not spent productively. In such cases, output falls, and even relatively small dollar volumes of unavailable supply can have an outsized influence on the economy. Fortunately, the development of global crude oil markets and deregulated domestic retail markets have made widespread petroleum product rationing a thing of the past, outside of occasional temporary regional events stemming from weather-related supply chain disruptions. Such events can have significant, even life-threatening impacts on the individuals involved, and minimizing those impacts through improving supply chain resilience is an important goal (and indeed is a central topic of the Department of Energy's Quadrennial Energy Review), but their temporary nature and regional scope means that the macroeconomic impact of the resulting petroleum product unavailability is limited.

Empirical Analysis of Energy Price Shocks

This section presents reduced-form empirical evidence on the relative importance of the different channels of energy supply shocks on the U.S. economy and on the changing correlations among energy prices. The results of this analysis suggest that a lower share of net oil imports in GDP enhances the resilience of the economy to oil price shocks.

The changing sensitivity of the U.S. economy to oil price shocks

The wealth channel makes the concrete prediction that the effect of an oil price shock on GDP growth scales with the share of GDP spent on net oil imports. The scaling of the other channels is less clear without a formal model, but generally those channels would arguably scale either with the importance of oil in the economy (for example, with the consumption expenditure share as examined by Edelstein and Kilian [2009]) or simply affect output directly. For example, the supply-side channels associated with temporary changes in factor prices would depend on elasticities of substitution among factors of production and their shares in production, not shares of net imports, while the uncertainty channel could depend on the overall importance of energy in the economy. If net imports were zero, the wealth effect channel would disappear, but the other channels would still exist.

These observations suggest an empirical strategy in which the effect of the shock is allowed to depend flexibly on the net oil import share, where the degree of dependence is estimated. In addition, the empirical strategy needs to take account of the fact that the effect of an oil shock plays out over a period of many quarters, not all at once. Accordingly, we consider a family of specifications in which an oil price shock has an effect on GDP over several quarters or, equivalently, GDP is affected by current and past values of the oil shock. This suggests the distributed lag model,

$$y_t = c_0 + \sum_{i=0}^{k} c_i \left[\alpha s_{t-i} + (1-\alpha)\mu \right] p_{t-i} + u_t , \qquad (1)$$

where y_t is the percentage growth of GDP, p_t is the oil price shock expressed as percent change, s_t is the net oil import expenditure share and μ is its mean, $c_0,...,c_k$ and α are parameters to be estimated, k is the number of lags, and u_t denotes the other factors determining GDP growth that are not considered in the model. If α = 1, then the price shock scales by the share, consistent with the wealth channel, whereas if α = 0 then the price shock does not vary over time with the share, consistent with the other channels being more important. Note that in the specification (1), if α = 1 and the net import share is zero, oil price shocks have no effect on GDP growth.

To estimate specification (1), we use quarterly data from 1960Q1 – 2006Q4 on real GDP growth, the narrow-concept expenditure share trend in Figure 3-2, and five measures of oil price shocks.[7] Because the oil price increased throughout 2007, peaking in July 2008 just months before the financial crisis, the estimation ends in 2006Q4 so as to avoid overstating oil price effects. The first two oil price shock variables are the quarterly percent change in two oil price measures: the crude petroleum producer price index as used by Hamilton (1996, 2003, 2009) (quarterly average of monthly data) and the spot price of West Texas Intermediate crude ("WTI", collected by the Energy Information Administration; quarterly average of monthly data). Although movements in oil prices are sometimes conveniently treated as exogenous, oil prices respond to economic conditions and there is a large, thoughtful literature that tackles the problems posed by this potential endogeneity (see for example Bernanke, Gertler, and Watson [1997], Barsky and Kilian [2002], Hamilton [2009], Kilian [2008b, 2009], and Ramey and Vine [2010]). The next two measures therefore aim to isolate exogenous movements in oil prices, thereby to reduce the chance of p_t being correlated with the other shock that comprise u_t in specification (1): Hamilton's (1996) net oil price increase variable, which is the percent by which the crude oil producer price index surpasses its previous 12-quarter peak, and zero if it does not (aggregated to the quarterly level as in Hamilton [2009]), and Ramey and Vine's (2010) oil shock variable, which is the residual from a regression of time-adjusted gasoline prices on four current and past macroeconomic variables and thereby aims to capture the exogenous gasoline expenditure shock associated with a potentially endogenous oil price hike (monthly shocks aggregated to quarterly; available 1964-2013).

The final shock variable measures *ex-ante* volatility of oil prices, not the level, and thus pertains to the supply-side and uncertainty channels; specifically, this series measures volatility as estimated using a GARCH(1,1) model of the percentage change of the monthly WTI spot price (estimated on monthly data 1947-2013, aggregated to quarterly by averaging).[8] This measure,

---

[7] The narrow-concept share is available for the full time span, whereas the broader-concept share is available only since 1973. The trend shown in in Figure 3-2 is used to avoid conflating the share with the oil price shock variable with which it is interacted in equation (1).

[8] Time series investigations into the macroeconomic effect of oil price volatility using GARCH and/or stochastic volatility approaches include Elder and Serletis (2010) and Jo (2014).

plotted in Figure 3-3, shows considerable variation, with the greatest percentage volatility occurring in the 1970s and before and during the 2007 recession, and relative quiescence during the mid- and late-1990s.

Figure 3-3
Estimated Ex-Ante Volatility of Oil Prices

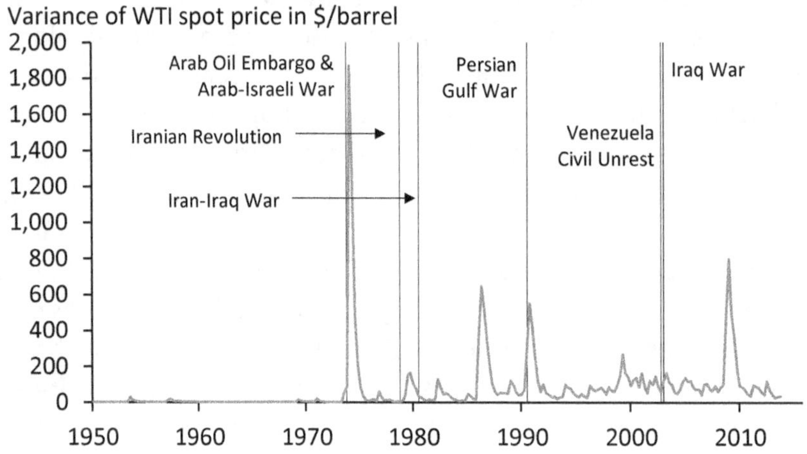

Source: EIA; CEA calculations

The results of estimation of the distributed lag specification (1) for GDP growth and consumption growth using eight lags are summarized in Table 3-2. The table presents estimated values of α, a test of the joint significance of the distributed lag coefficients, and a test of the significance of the 6-quarter cumulative effect; the coefficients themselves are not reported to save space. For GDP growth, for all oil variables except for the Hamilton net oil price increase, the estimated value of α is one, so that for the oil variables and the Ramey-Vine shock the effect of an oil price shock on GDP is proportional to the net import share, which varies over time. In all cases, the estimated effects are negative as expected, typically increasing in magnitude over the first 3-6 quarters. In addition, the dynamic effects are jointly statistically significant and the cumulative 6-quarter effect is individually statistically significant for all dependent variables. The results are similar for consumption growth.

Table 3-2: Empirical Results

Dependent Variable: Real GDP					
Price Shock Variable	WTI (%change)	PPI-Crude (%change)	Hamilton (1996) Price Shock	Ramey-Vine Shock	WTI Volatility
Shock Scale Parameter, α	1	1	0.224	1	1
Standard Error	--	--	0.346	--	--
P-value of F-test of all lag coefficients	<0.0001	<0.0001	<0.0001	<0.0001	<0.0001
T-test of 6-quarter Cumulative Effect	-2.14	-2.62	-3.17	-1.87	-2.45
P-value	0.034	0.009	0.002	0.063	0.015

Dependent Variable: Real PCE					
Price Shock Variable	WTI (%change)	PPI-Crude (%change)	Hamilton (1996) Price Shock	Ramey-Vine Shock	WTI Volatility
Shock Scale Parameter, α	1	1	0.342	1	1
Standard Error	--	--	0.332	--	--
P-value of F-test of all lag coefficients	<0.0001	<0.0001	<0.0001	<0.0001	<0.0001
T-test of 6-quarter Cumulative Effect	-3.34	-3.61	-3.91	-1.25	-2.30
P-value	0.001	<0.0001	0.0001	0.212	0.022

Note: Entries are results from estimation of the distributed lag model in Equation (1) by by nonlinear least squares, where α was parameterized using a logistic transformation to impose $0 \leq \alpha \leq 1$. Standard errors in the distributed lag specifications are autocorrelation robust. Standard errors for α are given only for interior estimates because of changes in sampling distributions at the boundary.

In economic terms, the variation over time of the effect of an oil shock on GDP growth implied by the estimated share specifications is substantial. Figure 3-4 shows the estimated dynamic effect on real GDP of a ten percent increase in the WTI spot price, estimated over the full data set (this is the so-called impulse response function associated with the estimated specification for WTI summarized in Table 3-2). For example, when the expenditure share is 2.2 percent, approximately its value at its peaks in 1980 and 2007, the time-series estimates imply that a ten percent increase in the price of oil is associated with a 0.5 percent fall in GDP after 6 quarters. In contrast, when the expenditure share is 0.9 percent, approximately its value in the mid-1990s, this effect on GDP is roughly -0.2 percent. Because the net petroleum import share was substantially lower in second half of 1980s through 1990s than in the late 1970s and early 1980s, these findings are consistent with the reduced effect of oil shocks on GDP found from the mid-1980s through the end of the century (for example, Hooker [1996], Nordhaus [2007], Blanchard-Galí [2010]).

Figure 3-4
Estimated Cumulative Effect a 10% Oil Price Shock on GDP

Quarters after shock

Percent change in GDP

Source: EIA; CEA calculations.

Taking these estimates at face value for the moment, they are somewhat larger than would be suggested by the wealth channel alone: for a net oil import share of 2.2 percent, the direct wealth effect of a 10 percent increase in oil prices would be to reduce GDP by 0.22 percent. Even with a Keynesian demand multiplier of 1.5, the reduction would be only 0.33 percent, or roughly two-thirds of the estimated 0.5 percent reduction. Although the estimated 0.5 percent reduction is within a 95% confidence interval of 0.33, these estimates are consistent with meaningful contributions by channels beyond the wealth effect.

The net expenditure share is currently relatively high in historical terms, at 1.8 percent, but is declining sharply. Because of declining demand for transportation fuel and increasing domestic production, the net expenditure share is projected to fall to the historically low level of 1 percent by 2017 under the AEO 2014 reference case. For the oil price specifications reported in Table 3-2, this projected decline in the net oil import share corresponds to large reductions of the sensitivity of the U.S. economy to oil price shocks.

These results are robust to changes in the estimation sample and to alternative econometric specifications, and aside from the Hamilton net oil price increase are robust to alternative shock measures.[9] Still, they are subject to a number of caveats. Most importantly, oil price changes can occur for multiple reasons, including response to increasing demand; that is, oil price changes are in general not exogenous, so the impulse response functions displayed in Figure 3-4 (or those obtained using the other oil price variables in Table 3-2) should be viewed as describing dynamic

---

[9] The results in Table 3-2 and the corresponding impulse response functions are robust to using instead the autoregressive-distributed lag model with four lags used by Hamilton (2003, 2008), to using a 12-lag distributed lag model (although statistical significance suffers with the added coefficients), to starting the estimation sample in 1954, to ending the estimation sample in 2013, and to using GDP and consumption growth deviated from a long-term cyclically adjusted estimate of their potential growth rates. The estimated impulse response functions are also robust to using instead a bivariate autoregressions with oil ordered causally first as in Edelstein and Kilian (2009), in which the oil price variable is $[\alpha s_t + (1-\alpha)\mu]p_t$ using the estimated value of α reported in Table 3-2.

correlations and not as causal effects. Identifying causal effects of oil price shocks is a central challenge of this literature, and doing so requires a credible strategy to isolate exogenous variation in the shocks. Identification approaches include formulating multivariate models which embed identifying assumptions (e.g. Bernanke, Gertler, and Watson [1997], Blanchard and Galí [2010], Kilian [2009], Baumeister and Peersman [2013], Kilian and Murphy [2014]) or using an instrumental variables approach (Hamilton [2003], Stock and Watson [2012]). The task of merging the variable-share specification with those approaches to identification is left to further work. Additionally, while the findings here point towards declining oil import shares as being an important reason for the reduced macroeconomic effect of oil price shocks, they do not rule out other factors, such as a changing mix of supply and demand shocks (e.g. Kilian [2009]), as contributing to this reduction. Finally, although the oil shock enters the specifications here nonlinearly in that it is interacted with a function of the share, this analysis does not examine whether these results resolve the findings in the literature on nonlinear oil price effects (see Hamilton [2010], Kilian and Vigfusson [2014], and Kilian [2014] for a review). For all these reasons, the results in Table 3.2 should be viewed as suggestive.

Energy supply diversification and falling correlations among U.S. energy prices

This empirical work so far has focused on the role of oil in macroeconomic energy security. Another aspect of macroeconomic energy security is the extent to which oil price changes produce broader movements in energy prices. Preliminary empirical evidence suggests that, for the United States, the boom in natural gas production has contributed to an attenuation of the link between oil price changes and other energy price changes.

As discussed above, the boom in nonconventional gas production detached the Henry Hub wholesale natural gas price from oil prices (Figure 2-15a). This detachment of the levels of the prices is also reflected in a reduced correlation of price changes. For the five years from 2001-2005, the correlation between monthly percent changes in the Henry Hub price and the WTI spot price was 0.43. From 2006-2010, this correlation fell to 0.19, and for the four years from 2010 to the present it is -0.17. Consistent with the declining correlation between oil and natural gas prices, the correlation between oil prices and wholesale electricity prices fell from 0.16 during 2000-2005 and 0.27 during 2006-2010 to -0.10 during 2010 to the present.

Discussion

Oil price shocks affect the economy through many channels. In addition to the wealth effect, those channels include shifts in the composition of domestic consumption, adjustments by firms facing a shift in the relative costs of their inputs, and reduced demand from heightened uncertainty. As Edelstein and Kilian (2009) emphasize, oil price shocks depress consumer sentiment. And, because gasoline is needed for routine transportation, oil price shocks are regressive.

Nevertheless, these results support the view that U.S. macroeconomic energy security is enhanced by reducing net petroleum imports, and they underscore the importance of reducing the dependence of the U.S. economy on petroleum. Recently, the net import share has been declining for a combination of reasons: declining demand for transportation fuels, increased domestic oil production combined with increasing refined product exports, and increasing use of biofuels. Thus further contributions to macroeconomic energy security can come from further improvements in fuel economy, as supported by the light- and heavy-vehicle standards; from reducing petroleum demand by shifting to natural gas and electricity as transportation energy sources; from supporting additional, environmentally responsible domestic oil production; and from further use of advanced, low-greenhouse gas biofuels.

IV.   A Path to a Low-Carbon Future

A central challenge of energy and environmental policy is to find a responsible path that balances the economic benefits of low-cost energy, the social and environmental costs associated with energy production, and our duty to future generations. As part of the United Nations Climate Change Conferences in Copenhagen and Cancún, the United States pledged to cut its carbon dioxide (CO_2) and other greenhouse gas emissions in the range of 17 percent below 2005 levels by 2020. Approximately 87 percent of U.S. anthropogenic emissions of all greenhouse gases (primarily CO_2 and methane) are energy-related, and fossil-fuel combustion accounts for approximately 94 percent of U.S. CO_2 emissions (EPA 2010).

From an economist's perspective, greenhouse gas emissions impose costs on others who are not involved in the transaction that creates the emissions; that is, greenhouse gas emissions generate a negative externality, of which much is borne by future generations. Appropriate policies to address this negative externality would internalize the externality, so that the price of emissions reflects their true cost, or would seek technological solutions that would similarly reduce the externality. Such policies incentivize energy efficiency and clean energy production.

In his 2013 State of the Union address, the President called on Congress to pass legislation that would provide a market-based mechanism for reducing emissions. Congress has failed to act but the Administration has other tools with which to deploy low-carbon technologies, including tax incentives for investment in and production of clean energy, and direct regulation of greenhouse gas (GHG) emissions, such as the 2012 light-duty fuel economy standards and the regulation of CO_2 emissions by fossil fuel fired electric generators under the Clean Air Act.[10]

The United States has made important progress in reducing GHG emissions. As Figure 4-1 shows, energy-related CO_2 emissions have fallen 10 percent from their peak in 2007. Given a counterfactual, or baseline, path for these variables, one can attribute the change in carbon emissions to a change in the carbon content of energy, a change in the rate of improvement of energy efficiency, and a change in the level of GDP, relative to the baseline path.[11]

---

[10] Regulations have costs and benefits, and computing the monetary benefits of reducing CO_2 emissions requires an estimate of the net present value of the cost of an additional, or marginal, ton of CO_2 emissions. This cost—which covers health, property damage, agricultural impacts, the value of ecosystem services, and other welfare costs of climate change—is often referred to as the "social cost of carbon" (SCC). In 2010, a Federal interagency working group, led by the Council of Economic Advisers and the Office of Management and Budget, produced a white paper that outlined a methodology for estimating the SCC and provided numeric estimates (White House 2010). Since then, the SCC has been used at various stages of rulemaking by the Department of Transportation, the Environmental Protection Agency, and the Department of Energy. The SCC estimate is updated as the science and models underlying the SCC develop, and in November 2013 public comments were invited on the most recent update of the SCC.

[11] Specifically, CO_2 emissions are the product of $(CO_2/Btu) \times (Btu/GDP) \times GDP$, where CO_2 represents U.S. CO_2 emissions in a given year, Btu represents energy consumption in that year, and GDP is that year's GDP. Taking logarithms of this expression, and then subtracting the actual values from the baseline, gives a decomposition of the CO_2 reduction into contributions from clean energy, energy efficiency, and the recession.

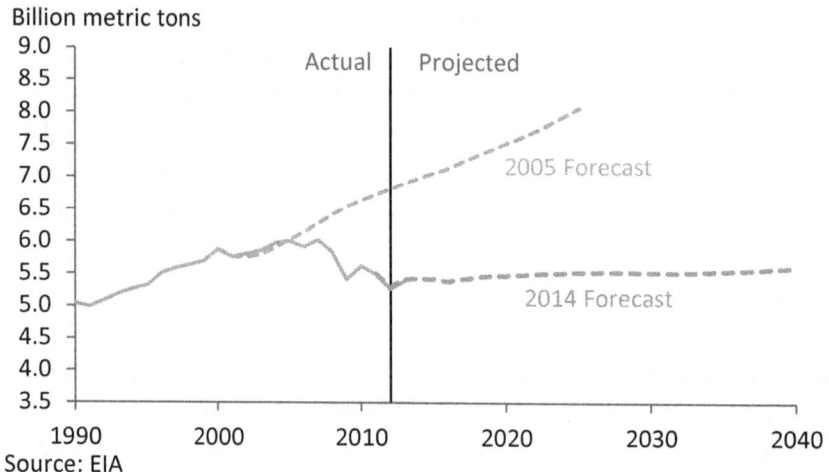

Figure 4-1
Energy-Related Carbon Dioxide Emissions

Billion metric tons

Actual | Projected

2005 Forecast

2014 Forecast

Source: EIA

The baseline path is computed using a combination of historical trends and published forecasts as of 2005. Relative to this baseline, slightly more than half of the decline is due to slower growth than projected in 2005, that is, because of the decline in economic activity as a result of the Great Recession. Slightly less than half the reduction is due to cleaner energy, primarily the reduction in electricity generated by coal and the increase in cleaner natural gas and zero-emissions wind and solar generation. Improvements in energy efficiency made a small contribution: although economy-wide efficiency improved over this period, it improved only slightly faster than the rate projected by the Energy Information Administration in 2005. This analysis of the recent reduction in emissions shows that while progress has been made, much more remains to be done.

The All-of-the-Above energy strategy develops and deploys low-carbon technologies and lays the foundation for a clean energy future. This support ranges from research and experimentation funding for new energy technologies to supporting large-scale deployment. The transition to a low-carbon future is also supported through direct regulation of carbon emissions under the authority of the Clean Air Act, and the Environmental Protection Agency is developing regulations to reduce CO_2 emissions from fossil fuel electric generating units as part of the President's Climate Action Plan.

Reducing Emissions through Improved Efficiency

The amount of energy used to produce a dollar of real GDP has declined steadily over the past four decades, and today stands at less than half of what it was in 1970 (Figure 4-2). This improvement in overall energy efficiency, which has averaged 1.5 percent per year since 1960, is due in part to more efficient use of energy resources to complete the same or similar tasks, and in part to shifts in the types of tasks undertaken. Figure 4-2 also presents the Economy-Wide Energy Intensity Index developed by the Department of Energy, which estimates the amount of energy needed to produce a basket of goods in one year, relative to the previous year. Between 1985 and 2011, the DOE Energy Intensity Index fell by 14 percent. In contrast, the energy-GDP ratio fell by 36 percent. Thus, while much of the decline in energy usage per dollar of GDP has come from improvements in energy efficiency, much of it has also come from other factors such as shifts in the composition of output, in particular shifts from more to less energy-intensive sectors of the economy.

Figure 4-2
U.S. Energy Intensity, 1950-2011

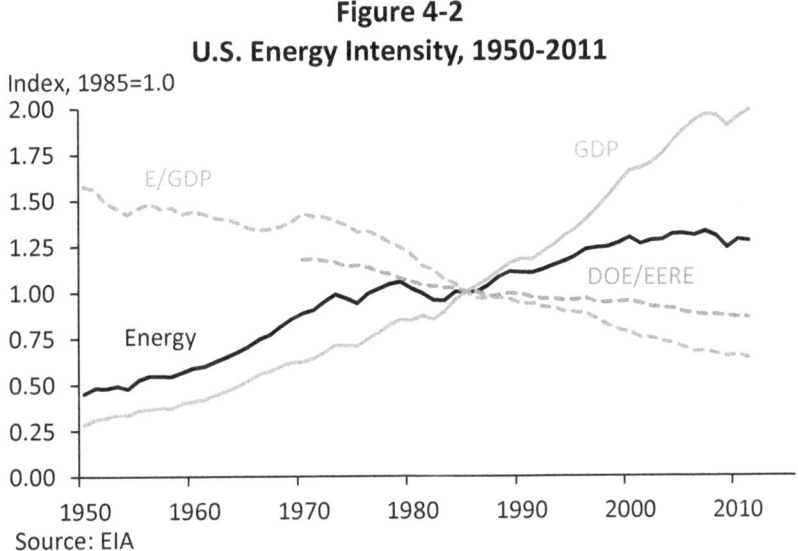

Source: EIA

Both market forces and government programs spur energy efficiency improvements. For example, as Figure 4-3a shows, gasoline demand per capita rose through the early 2000s and plateaued in the mid-2000s before dropping substantially during the recession. As the economy recovered, however, gasoline demand per capita continued to fall. Some of this continued decline in gasoline demand stems from the relatively high real gasoline prices shown in Figure 4-3a, but that is only a partial explanation. Increasing fuel efficiency brought about by Federal fuel economy standards also played a role. In 2012, the Administration finalized fuel economy standards that, together with the Administration's first round of standards, will nearly double from 2010 levels the fuel economy of light duty vehicles to the equivalent of 54.5 miles per gallon by the 2025 model year (Figure 4-3b). Furthermore, beginning in model year 2014, medium- and heavy-duty trucks must meet new energy efficiency standards as well, which are projected to increase their fuel efficiency by 10 to 20 percent by 2018.

As mentioned earlier in this report, the Administration has also undertaken a number of other initiatives as part of its All-of-the-Above Energy Strategy to boost energy efficiency in buildings, appliances, and its own operations.

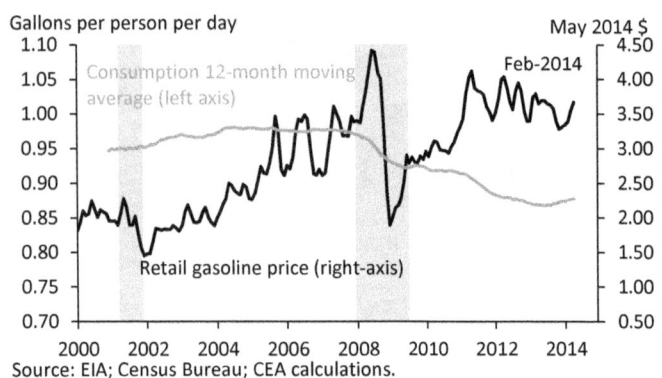

Figure 4-3a
U.S. Per Capita Gasoline Consumption

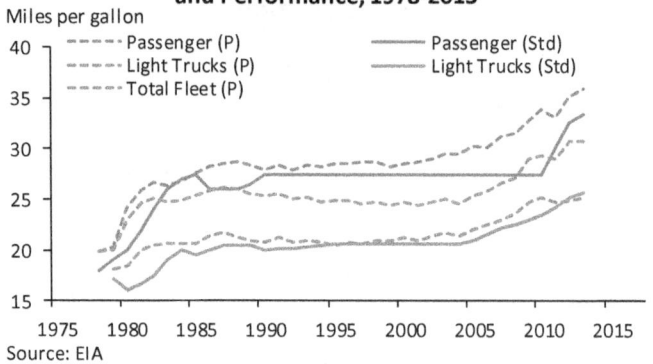

Figure 4-3b
Corporate Average Fuel Economy Standard
and Performance, 1978-2013

Source: EIA; Census Bureau; CEA calculations.

Source: EIA

Natural Gas as a Transitional Fuel

Natural gas is already playing a central role in the transition to a clean energy future. According to the decomposition mentioned above, nearly half of the CO_2 emissions reductions from 2005 to 2013 came from fuel switching, primarily switching from the use of coal to natural gas, wind, and solar for the purpose of generating electricity. Nonconventional natural gas development has opened a vast resource, and, as shown in Figure 4-4, the Energy Information Administration projects increasing quantities of natural gas production along with low prices over the coming two decades.

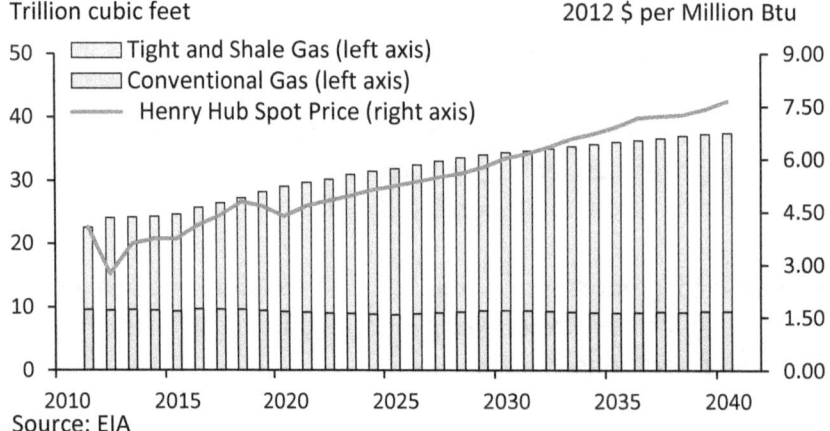

Figure 4-4
U.S. Natural Gas Production and
Wholesale Prices, 2011-2040

Source: EIA

A leading reason for the increased use of natural gas for electricity production is that its price fell. As Figure 4-5 shows, the decline in natural gas prices in 2008-9 and in 2012 induced substitution of natural gas for coal in electricity generation. In 2013, the benchmark natural gas price increased from $3.33 per mmBtu in January 2013 to $4.24 per mmBtu in December 2013, and as natural gas prices rose relative to coal, the use of coal for electricity generation increased while the use of natural gas decreased. Looking ahead, the relatively low price of natural gas will make it an economically attractive alternative fuel as regulation of CO_2 and other emissions under the Clean Air Act further reduces coal-fired electricity generation.

Figure 4-5
Change in Monthly Electricity Generation and Prices

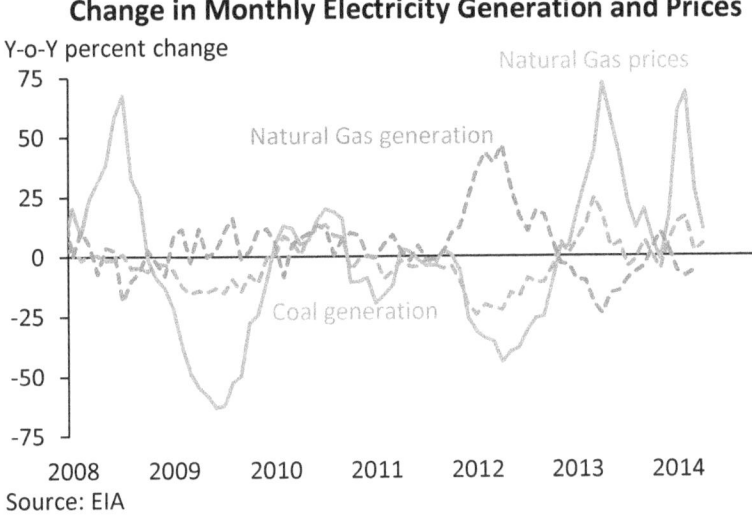

Source: EIA

It is important that this expansion of natural gas production be done responsibly and with environmental safeguards. Environmental concerns associated with natural gas include fugitive methane emissions (methane is a potent greenhouse gas), flaring, and local environmental issues associated with water and land use for hydraulic fracturing operations. As part of the Climate Action Plan, the Administration is undertaking a strategy both to reduce methane emissions and to address gaps in current data on methane emissions. The regulatory structure for addressing local environmental concerns, especially around land and water use, exists primarily at the state and local level. Research that will inform prudent local environmental regulation of hydraulic fracturing is actively under way.

Looking further ahead, developing natural gas generation infrastructure now prepares for future widespread deployment of wind and solar generation. Wind and solar are non-dispatchable because of variable wind speeds and insolation, so both need either storage or backup generation capacity. Developing base load natural gas infrastructure today facilitates its use tomorrow for peak demand and renewable backup generation.

Supporting Renewables, Nuclear, and Clean Coal
Low- and zero-carbon renewable, nuclear, and clean coal energy sources have a central role to play in a clean energy future. Consequently, the President's All-of-the-Above strategy makes a strong commitment to supporting these technologies.

Wind and solar generation are zero-emission sources of energy and thus do not create a negative climate externality. If emissions were priced to internalize the climate externality, then, wind, solar, and other renewable energy sources would therefore enjoy an additional price advantage beyond current market prices. In the absence of market-based mechanisms to internalize the externality, it is appropriate to provide support through tax incentives and other measures commensurate with the value of the GHG reductions provided by those zero-emissions energy sources. Accordingly, the Administration backs such support for renewables, including the renewable energy production tax credit. In addition, the Administration supports early deployment projects aimed at bringing down the ultimate market price of renewables.

Government support, increasing competitiveness of wind and photovoltaic electricity production, and renewable portfolio standards that many states have adopted have together increased the share of electricity generated by non-hydro renewables from roughly 2 percent in 2007 to 6 percent in 2013 (Figure 4-6). Since the beginning of 2011, the average cost of solar panels has dropped more than 60 percent and since the beginning of 2010 the cost of a solar photovoltaic electric system has dropped by about 50 percent.

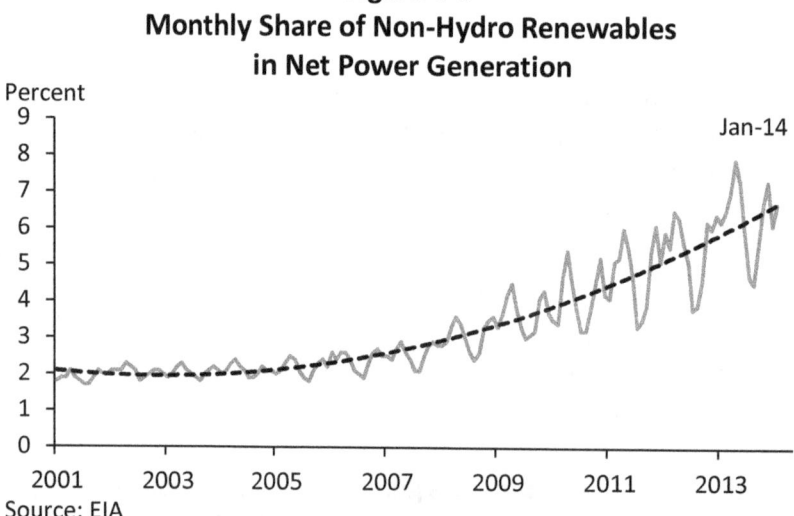

Figure 4-6
Monthly Share of Non-Hydro Renewables
in Net Power Generation

Source: EIA

The Administration has also supported solar deployment. Five years ago, there were no renewable energy projects on public lands. Today, the Interior Department is on track to permit enough renewable energy projects on public lands by 2020 to power more than six million homes; the Defense Department has set a goal to deploy three gigawatts of renewable energy – including solar, wind, biomass, and geothermal – on Army, Navy, and Air Force installations by 2025; and, as part of the Climate Action Plan, the Federal Government overall has committed to sourcing 20 percent of the energy consumed in Federal buildings from renewable sources by 2020.

Other Renewables

The Administration's All-of-the-Above Energy Strategy also includes other forms of electricity and thermal generation from renewables, including hydropower and geothermal energy. Electricity production from conventional hydropower was 5 percent higher in 2013 than in 2008, although trends in hydropower from year to year depend on water availability. In 2013, President Obama signed two laws aimed at boosting hydropower, in part through encouraging hydropower development at non-powered dams. Similarly, electricity production from geothermal power grew from 2008 to 2013, and the Department of Energy funds research in a number of areas, including enhanced geothermal systems, that hold promise for developing these resources in the future. Finally, the Energy Department funds research in energy storage for applications ranging from better batteries for electric vehicles to energy storage technologies with potential grid-scale applications. Innovations in energy storage can enhance electricity system reliability and resilience, and enable both greater adoption of renewable energy resources and more effective utilization of the existing electric system.

Nuclear and Clean Coal

Nuclear energy provides zero-carbon base load electricity, and through the Energy Department the Administration is supporting nuclear research and deployment. A high priority of the Department has been to help accelerate the timelines for the commercialization and deployment of small modular reactor (SMR) technologies through the SMR Licensing Technical Support program. Small modular reactors offer the advantage of lower initial capital investment, scalability, and siting flexibility at locations unable to accommodate more traditional larger reactors. They also have the potential for enhanced safety and security, for example through built-in passive safety systems. In December 2013, the Energy Department announced an award to support a new project to design, certify and help commercialize SMRs.

The Energy Department is also supporting deployment of advanced large-scale reactors. In February 2014, the Department of Energy issued $6.5 billion in loan guarantees to support the construction of the nation's next generation of advanced nuclear reactors. The two new 1,100-megawatt reactors, which will be located in Georgia, feature advanced safety components and could provide a standardized design for the U.S. utilities market.

The Administration is also advancing clean coal technology. The Department of Energy's clean coal R&D is focused on developing and demonstrating advanced power generation and carbon capture, utilization and storage technologies by increasing overall system efficiencies and reducing capital costs. In the near-term, advanced technologies that increase the power generation efficiency for new plants and technologies to capture CO_2 are being developed. In the longer term, the goal is to increase energy plant efficiencies and reduce both the energy and capital costs of CO_2 capture and storage from new, advanced coal plants and existing plants. As part of its nearly $6 billion commitment to clean coal technology, the Administration, partnered with industry, has already invested in four commercial-scale and 24 industrial-scale CCS projects that together will store more than 15 million metric tons of CO_2 per year and, through oilfield injection, will support production of more than 37.5 million barrels of oil per year.

Renewables also must play an important role in the transportation sector. Promising low-emission alternatives include hybrids, electric vehicles, hydrogen, natural gas, and biofuels. The effective emissions from an electric vehicle depend on the source of electricity, and will fall as the electric power sector reduces its CO_2 emissions. Different fuels are likely to be relatively better suited for different needs, for example natural gas for busses and heavy-duty fleet vehicles and electricity for private vehicles in urban settings. But the transformation of the transportation sector is in its infancy, so energy policy needs to support research and development of a wide range of advanced transportation fuel options.

The convenience of high energy content liquid fuels means that their role in the transportation sector could persist for decades. If so, renewable liquid fuels with a low GHG footprint would prove important for reducing the climate impact of the transportation sector. Already, the U.S. transportation sector uses ethanol, biodiesel, renewable diesel, and lesser quantities of other renewable fuels. Ethanol is used as a replacement for MTBE to boost octane and is blended into nearly all of the U.S. gasoline supply as E10, which is 10 percent ethanol by volume. Demand for renewable transportation fuels is further supported by the Renewable Fuel Standard (RFS). To qualify under the RFS as conventional renewable fuel, the fuel must achieve a 20 percent life cycle GHG emissions reduction, relative to petroleum gasoline. The legislation authorizing the Renewable Fuel Standard, which was expanded under the Energy Independence and Security Act of 2007, envisioned conventional fuels such as corn ethanol to be transitional and, based on EIA projections at the time, these conventional renewables would constitute a declining share of the total fuel consumption. As Figure 4-7 shows, blending of ethanol into E10 has already reduced the amount of petroleum in gasoline substantially. The long-term environmental goal of the RFS is to support the development of advanced biofuels, which have life cycle GHG emissions reductions of at least 50 percent, and especially to support cellulosic biofuels (which use feedstocks such as corn stover) with GHG emissions reductions of at least 60 percent.

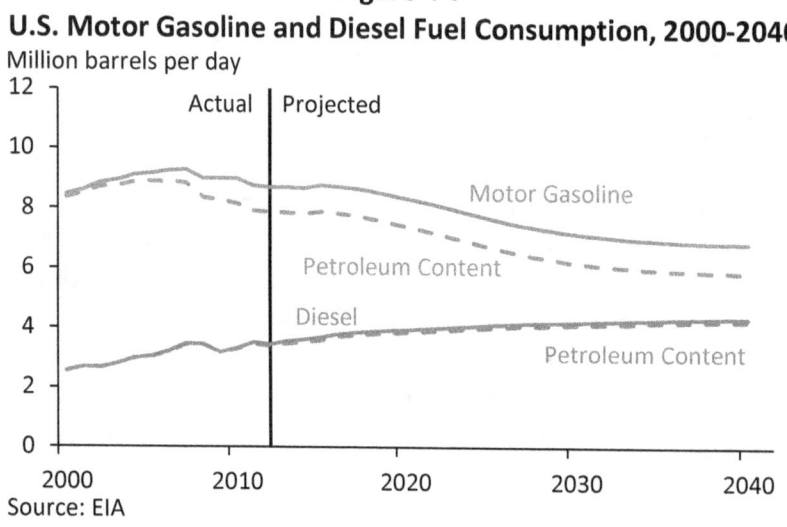

Figure 4-7
U.S. Motor Gasoline and Diesel Fuel Consumption, 2000-2040
Source: EIA

From 2005 to 2011 (the last year of data), the United States reduced its total carbon pollution more than any other nation on Earth. The United States is further reducing its GHG emissions through improved energy efficiency, taking advantage of nonconventional natural gas as a transitional fuel, supporting renewable, nuclear, and clean coal energy sources, and regulation under the Clean Air Act. Nevertheless, curbing GHG emissions, like climate change, is ultimately an international challenge. The United States currently produces approximately 15 percent of global carbon emissions, second to China (Figure 4-8). As the economies in the developing world expand, their energy needs will increase, and business-as-usual projections indicate that an increasing share of GHG emissions will come from outside the United States and from the developing world in particular.

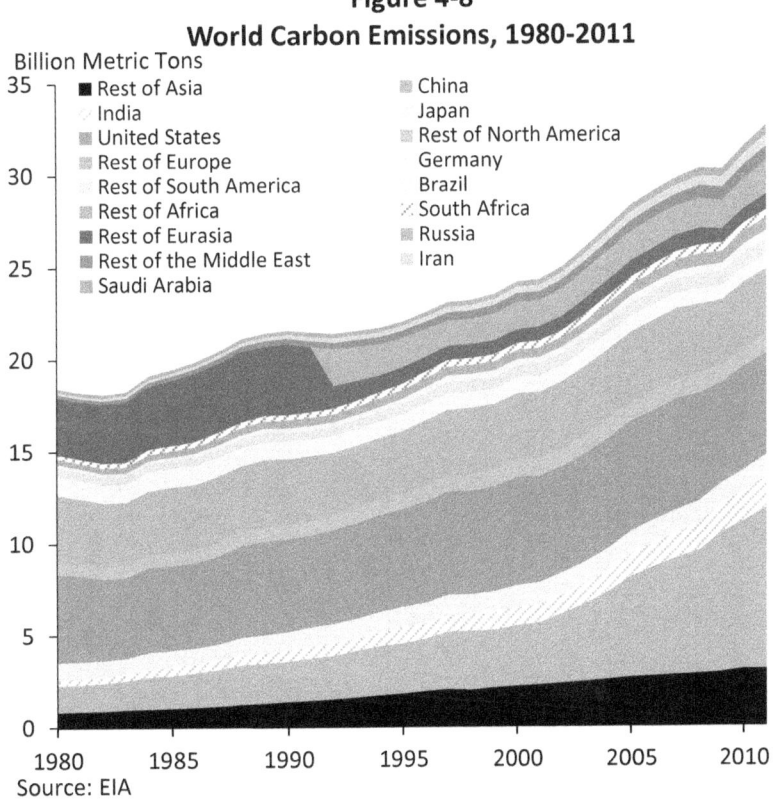

Figure 4-8
World Carbon Emissions, 1980-2011

Source: EIA

While some might suggest that the growing international share of GHG emissions means that U.S. reductions are too small to matter, in fact the opposite is true. U.S. leadership is vital to the success of international negotiations to set meaningful reduction goals. This leadership is multifaceted. Through low-carbon technologies developed and demonstrated in the United States (including nonconventional natural gas technologies), the United States can help the rest of the world reduce its dependence on coal. The President's initiative under the Climate Action Plan to lead efforts to eliminate international public financing for new conventional coal plants, except in the poorest countries without economically feasible alternatives, will further help the world move towards cleaner fuels for electric power. Investing in research in new technologies such as carbon capture and storage for clean coal, natural gas, biomass co-firing, and advanced renewable liquid fuels pushes forward these frontiers, supports U.S. technology leadership in clean energy, and advances technologies that will provide global benefits. And by taking strong steps to reduce emissions at home, through new initiatives such as the second round of heavy duty vehicle fuel economy standards, programs to reduce methane emissions, and regulation of CO_2 emissions from fossil fuel fired generators, the Administration is in a much stronger position to secure similar commitments from other nations. The combination of these efforts is laying the foundation for a cleaner energy future that is economically efficient, upholds our responsibility to future generations, and provides positive net economic benefits.

References

Barsky, Robert B., and Lutz Kilian. 2002. "Do We Really Know That Oil Caused the Great Stagflation? A Monetary Alternative." *NBER Macroeconomics Annual 2001,* vol. 16, pp. 137–83.

Baumeister, Christiane and Gert Peersman. 2013. "Time-Varying Effects of Oil Supply Shocks on the U.S. Economy." *American Economic Journal: Macroeconomics*, vol. 5, pp. 1-28.

Bernanke, Ben S. 1983. "Irreversibility, Uncertainty, and Cyclical Investment." *Quarterly Journal of Economics*, vol. 98, pp. 85-106.

Bernanke, Ben S., Mark Gertler, and Mark Watson. 1997. "Systematic Monetary Policy and the Effects of Oil Price Shocks." *Brookings Papers on Economic Activity,* no. 1: 91–142.

Blanchard, Olivier J., and Jordi Galí. 2010. "The Macroeconomic Effects of Oil Price Shocks: Why Are the 2000s So Different from the 1970s?" In *International Dimensions of Monetary Policy,* edited by Jordi Galí and Mark J.Gertler. University of Chicago Press.

Blinder, Alan. 2009. "Comment on Hamilton, Causes and Consequences of the Oil Shock of 2007-08." *Brookings Papers on Economic Activity*, no. 1: 262-267.

Bloom, Nicholas. 2009. "The Impact of Uncertainty Shocks." *Econometrica* 77:623–85.

Cruz, Jennifer, Peter W. Smith, and Sara Stanley. 2014. "The Marcellus Shale Gas Boom in Pennsylvania: Employment and Wage Trends." *Bureau of Labor Statistics Monthly Labor Review*, February, at http://www.bls.gov/opub/mlr/2014/article/the-marcellus-shale-gas-boom-in-pennsylvania.htm

Council of Economic Advisers and Department of Energy. 2013. "Economic Benefits of Increasing Grid Resilience to Weather Outages."

Edelstein, Paul and Lutz Kilian. 2009. "How Sensitive are Consumer Expenditures to Retail Energy?" *Journal of Monetary Economics* 56, 766-779.

Elder, John and Apostolos Serletis. 2010. "Oil Price Uncertainty." *Journal of Money, Credit and Banking*, vol. 42, pp. 1137-1159.

Environmental Protection Agency.2010. "Inventory of U.S. Greenhouse Gas Emissions and Sinks: 1990-2010."
(http://www.epa.gov/climatechange/ghgemissions/usinventoryreport.html).

Hamilton, James D. 1983. "Oil and the Macroeconomy since World War II." *Journal of Political Economy* 91, no. 2: 228–48.

Hamilton, James D. 1988. "A Neoclassical Model of Unemployment and the Business Cycle." *Journal of Political Economy* 96, no. 3: 593–617.

Hamilton, James D. 1996. "This Is What Happened to the Oil Price-Macroeconomy Relationship." *Journal of Monetary Economics* 38, no. 2: 215–20.

Hamilton, James D. 2003. "What Is an Oil Shock?" *Journal of Econometrics* 113: 363–98.

Hamilton, James D. 2009. "Causes and Consequences of the Oil Shock of 2007–08." *Brookings Papers on Economic Activity,* no. 1: 215–83.

Hamilton, James D. 2010. "Nonlinearities and the Macroeconomic Effects of Oil Prices." Working Paper no. 16186. Cambridge, Mass.: National Bureau of Economic Research.

Hooker, Mark A. 1996. "What Happened to the Oil Price-Macroeconomy Relationship?" *Journal of Monetary Economics* 38: 195-213.

IHS CERA. October 2012. *America's New Energy Future: The Unconventional Oil and Gas Revolution and the U.S. Economy. Volume 1: National Economic Conditions*.

Interagency Working Group on Social Cost of Carbon, United States Government.2010. "Technical Support Document: - Social Cost of Carbon for Regulatory Impact Analysis Under Executive Order 12866".

Jo, Soojin. 2014. "The Effects of Oil Price Uncertainty on Global Real Economic Activity." manuscript, Bank of Canada; forthcoming, *Journal of Money, Credit and Banking*.

Kellogg, Ryan. 2010. "The Effect of Uncertainty on Investment: Evidence from Texas Oil Drilling." *NBER Working Paper* 16541.

Kilian, Lutz. 2008a. "Exogenous Oil Supply Shocks: How Big Are They and How Much Do They Matter for the U.S. Economy?" *Review of Economics and Statistics* 90, no. 2: 216–40.

Kilian, Lutz. 2008b. "The Economic Effect of Energy Price Shocks." *Journal of Economic Literature* 46, no. 4: 871–909.

Kilian, Lutz. 2009. "Not All Oil Price Shocks Are Alike: Disentangling Demand and Supply Shocks in the Crude Oil Market." *American Economic Review* 99, no. 3: 1053–69.

Kilian, Lutz. 2014. "Oil Price Shocks: Causes and Consequences." Forthcoming: *Annual Review of Resource Economics.*

Kilian, Lutz and Daniel P. Murphy. 2014. "The Role of Inventories and Speculative Trading in the Global Market for Crude Oil." *Journal of Applied Economics*, vol. 29, pp. 454-478.

Kilian, Lutz and Robert J. Vigfusson. 2014. "The Role of Oil Price Shocks in Causing U.S. Recessions." manuscript, University of Michigan.

Nordhaus, William D. 2007. "Who's Afraid of a Big Bad Oil Shock?" *BPEA,* no. 2:219–238.

Ramey, Valerie A., and Daniel J. Vine. 2010. "Oil, Automobiles, and the U.S. Economy: How Much Have Things Really Changed?" *NBER Macroeconomics Annual* 25: 333–67.

Stock, James H. and Mark W. Watson. 2012. "Disentangling the Channels of the 2007-09 Recession." *Brookings Papers on Economic Activity*, no. 1: 81-135.

www.ingramcontent.com/pod-product-compliance
Lightning Source LLC
Chambersburg PA
CBHW080619180526
45168CB00007B/2973